Helienke

go! CHINESE

听说读打写

GW00686284

GO 400

Textbook
(Simplified Character Edition)

罗秋昭
Julie LO

薛意梅
Emily YIH

CENGAGE Learning™

Andover • Melbourne • Mexico City • Stamford, CT • Toronto • Hong Kong • New Delhi • Seoul • Singapore • Tokyo

CENGAGE Learning™

Go! Chinese Go400 Textbook
(Simplified Character Edition)
Julie Lo, Emily Yih

Publishing Director, CLT Product Director:
Paul K. H. Tan

Editorial Manager:
Lan Zhao

Associate Development Editor:
Coco Koh

Editor:
Titus Teo

Senior Graphic Designer:
Melvin Chong

Senior Product Manager (Asia):
Joyce Tan

Product Manager (Outside Asia):
Mei Yun Loh

Assistant Publishing Manager:
Pauline Lim

Production Executive:
Cindy Chai

Account Manager (China):
Arthur Sun

Assistant Editor, ELT:
Yuan Ting Soh

For product information and technology assistance, contact us at
Cengage Learning Asia Customer Support, 65-6410-1200
For permission to use material from this text or product,
submit all requests online at **www.cengageasia.com/permissions**
Further permissions questions can be emailed to
asia.permissionrequest@cengage.com

ISBN-13: 978-981-4246-48-4
ISBN-10: 981-4246-48-4

Cengage Learning Asia Pte Ltd
5 Shenton Way #01-01
UIC Building
Singapore 068808

Cengage Learning is a leading provider of customized learning solutions with office locations around the globe, including Andover, Melbourne, Mexico City, Stamford (CT), Toronto, Hong Kong, New Delhi, Seoul, Singapore, and Tokyo. Locate your local office at **www.cengage.com/global**

Cengage Learning products are represented in Canada by Nelson Education, Ltd.

For product information, visit **www.cengageasia.com**

Photo credits
(Below photo-numbers only © 2010 Jupiterimages Corporation)
Cover: © Charly Franklin/Taxi/Getty Images. p. 2: (top to bottom, left to right) © Gloda/Dreamstime.com; 87464560; © Serdarbasak/Dreamstime.com; © Nexus7/Dreamstime.com; © Wirelessg/Dreamstime.com; © Blueice69caddy/Dreamstime.com; © iStockphoto.com/Steven Miric; © Monkeybusinessimages/Dreamstime.com; © Bernard van Berg/Iconia/Getty Images; p. 14: (top to bottom, except "Chinese") 90381244; © Moth/Dreamstime.com, 5236552; 92818659; 93152405; © Jaboardm/Dreamstime.com; © Monkeybusinessimages/Dreamstime.com; 93463348; p. 34: © iStockphoto.com/Steve Cole; p. 35: © iStockphoto.com/ Anastasia Pelikh; p. 38: (top to bottom, left to right) 93241368; 93889999; © Jcpsad/Dreamstime.com; 4826262; © Mikael Dubois/Johner Images/Getty Images; © Silverfish81/Dreamstime.com; © Steve Teague/Dorling Kindersley/Getty Images; © Purestock/Purestock/Getty Images; 87511061; © iStockphoto.com/ V. J. Matthew; © JooLee Koh; p. 54: (top to bottom) 87563126; © Yujiro/Dreamstime.com; p. 56: 92760353; p. 74: (top to bottom, left to right) 93607453; 92215677; © iStockphoto.com/bluestocking; © iStockphoto.com/bluestocking; 87496792; © Gbh007/Dreamstime.com; © iStockphoto.com/Natasha Litova; 92233361; 92190534; © iStockphoto.com/ ma-k; p. 86: (top to bottom, left to right) © Rechitansorin/Dreamstime.com; © Tashka/Dreamstime.com; 87795342; © Raytags/Dreamstime.com; © Bobitoshev/Dreamstime.com; 89480455; 93812372; 87465460; 90834057; © iStockphoto.com/Tomaz Levstek; p. 87: (left to right) © iStockphoto.com/narvikk; © iStockphoto.com/Bela Tibor Kozma; p. 95: © iStockphoto.com/Hippo Studio; p. 96: (left to right) © iStockphoto.com/Jennifer Trenchard; © iStockphoto.com/Ashok Rodrigues; p. 98: (top to bottom, left to right) © Orac/Dreamstime.com; 87451785; 93060284; 92748226; 87504414; © Pakhnyushchyy/Dreamstime.com; 87812696; 94264571; © Zzzdim/Dreamstime.com; © Fleyeing/Dreamstime.com; © iStockphoto.com/Amanda Rohde; p. 99: (top to bottom) © iStockphoto.com/GelatoPlus; 93235801; 87692229; 87467253; p. 110: (top to bottom; left to right) © Amberleaf/Dreamstime.com; 87800259; 87826185; © Monkeybusinessimages/Dreamstime.com; © Stockbyte/Stockbyte/Getty Images; 87790825; 87546010; © Wiseangel/Dreamstime.com; 87967339; 93433889.

Printed in Singapore
2 3 4 5 14 13 12 11

Acknowledgements

Go! Chinese is designed to be used together with ***IQChinese Go*** courseware, a series of multimedia CD-ROM developed by **IQChinese**. We sincerely thank **Wu, Meng-Tien** (Instruction Manager, IQChinese) and **Lanni Wang** (Instruction Specialist, IQChinese) for their tremendous editorial support and advice throughout the development of this program.

We also like to thank the following individuals who offered many helpful insights, ideas, and suggestions for improvement during the product development stage of ***Go! Chinese***.

- **Jessie Lin Brown**, Singapore American School, Singapore
- **Henny Chen**, Moreau Catholic High School, USA
- **Yeafen Chen**, University of Wisconsin-Milwaukee, USA
- **Christina Hsu**, Superior Education, USA
- **Yi Liang Jiang**, Beijing Language and Culture University, China
- **Yan Jin**, Singapore American School, Singapore
- **Kerman Kwan**, Irvine Chinese School, USA
- **Chi-Chien Lu**, IBPS Chinese School, USA
- **Andrew Scrimgeour**, University of South Australia, Australia
- **James L. Tan**, Grace Christian High School, the Philippines
- **Man Tao**, Koning Williem I College, the Netherlands
- **Chiungwen Tsai**, Westside Chinese School, USA
- **Tina Wu**, Westside High School, USA
- **YaWen (Alison) Yang**, Concordian International School, Thailand

Preface

Go! Chinese, together with ***IQChinese Go* multimedia CD-ROM**, is a fully-integrated Chinese language program that offers an easy, enjoyable, and effective learning experience for learners of Chinese as a foreign language.

The themes and lesson plans of the program are designed with reference to the American National Standards for Foreign Language Learning developed by ACTFL[1], and the Curriculum Guides for Modern Languages developed by the Toronto District Board of Education. The program aims to help beginners develop their communicative competence in the four language skills of listening, speaking, reading, and writing while gaining an appreciation of the Chinese culture, exercising their ability to compare and contrast different cultures, making connections with other discipline areas, and extending their learning experiences to their home and communities.

The program employs innovative teaching methodologies and computer applications to enhance language learning, as well as keep students motivated in and outside of the classroom. The CD-ROM companion gives students access to audio, visual, and textual information about the language all at once. Chinese typing is systematically integrated into the program to facilitate the acquisition and retention of new vocabulary and to equip students with a skill that is becoming increasingly important in the Internet era wherein more and more professional and personal correspondence is done electronically.

Course Design

The program is divided into two series: Beginner and Intermediate. The Beginner Series, which comprises four levels (Go100-400), provides a solid foundation for continued study of the Intermediate Series (Go500-800). Each level includes a student text, a workbook, and a CD-ROM companion.

Beginner Series: Go100 – Go400

Designed for zero beginners, each level of the Beginner Series is made up of 10 colorfully illustrated lessons. Each lesson covers new vocabulary and simple sentence structures with particular emphasis on listening and speaking skills. In keeping with the communicative approach, a good mix of activities such as role play, interviews, games, pair work, and language exchanges are incorporated to allow students to learn to communicate through interaction in the target language. The CD-ROM uses rhythmic chants, word games, quizzes, and Chinese typing exercises to improve students' pronunciation, mastery of *pinyin*, and their ability to recognize and read words and sentences taught in each lesson.

The Beginner Series can be completed in roughly 240 hours (160 hours on Textbook and 80 hours on CD-ROM). Upon completion of the Beginner Series, the student will have acquired approximately 500 Chinese characters and 1000 common phrases.

Intermediate Series: Go500 – Go800

The Intermediate Series continues with the use of the communicative approach, but places a greater emphasis on Culture, Community, and Comparison. Through stories revolving around Chinese-American families, students learn vocabulary necessary for expressing themselves in a variety of contexts, describing their world, and discussing cultural differences.

The Intermediate Series can be completed in roughly 320 hours (240 hours on Textbook and 80 hours on CD-ROM). Upon completion of both the Beginner and Intermediate Series, the student will have acquired approximately 1000 Chinese characters and 2400 common phrases.

[1] American Council on the Teaching of Foreign Languages (http://www.actfl.org)

Course Features

Vocabulary and Sentence Structures

The program places emphasis on helping students use the target language in contexts relevant to their everyday lives. Therefore, the chosen vocabulary and sentence structures are based on familiar topics such as family, school activities, hobbies, weather, shopping, food, pets, modes of transport, etc. The same topics are revisited throughout the series to reinforce learning, as well as to expand on the vocabulary and sentence structures acquired before.

Listening and Speaking

Communicative activities encourage and require a learner to speak with and listen to other learners. Well-designed and well-executed communicative activities can help turn the language classroom into an active and enjoyable place where learners are motivated to learn and can learn what they need. The program integrates a variety of communicative activities such as role play, interviews, games, pair work, and language exchanges to give students the opportunity to put what they have learned into practice.

Word Recognition and Reading

Each lesson introduces about 12 new Chinese characters. Using the spiral approach, each new character is first introduced and then recycled in classroom activities and subsequent lessons to enhance retention of new vocabulary over time. *Pinyin* (phonetic notation) is added above newly introduced characters so that students can learn to pronounce them. To make sure students do not become over-reliant on *pinyin* to read Chinese, repeated vocabulary is stripped of *pinyin* so that students can learn to recognize and read the actual written characters in due course. For the same reason, the CD-ROM companion does not display the *pinyin* of words automatically.

Type-to-Learn Methodology

The unique characteristic of this series is the use of Chinese typing as an instructional strategy to improve listening, pronunciation, and word recognition. Activities in the CD-ROM require students to type characters or sentences as they are read aloud or displayed on the computer screen. Students will be alerted if they make a mistake and will be given the chance to correct them. If they do not get it right on the third try, the software provides immediate feedback on how to correct the error. This interactive trial-and-error process allows students to develop self-confidence and learn the language by doing.

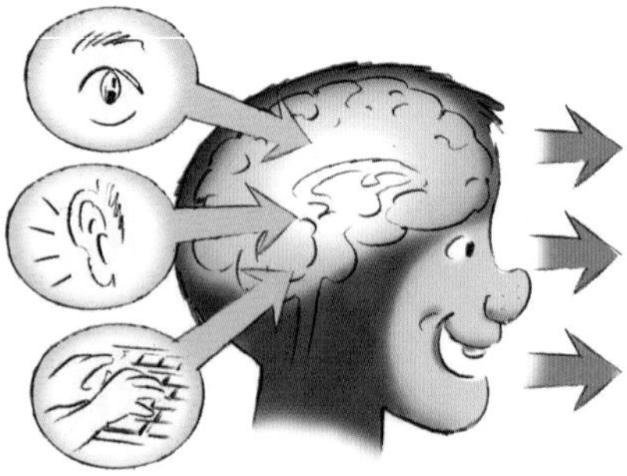

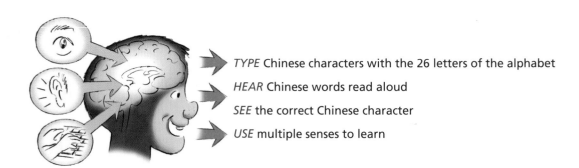

TYPE Chinese characters with the 26 letters of the alphabet

HEAR Chinese words read aloud

SEE the correct Chinese character

USE multiple senses to learn

Chinese Characters and Character Writing

The program does not require the student to be able to write all the core vocabulary; the teacher may however assign more character writing practice according to his or her classroom emphasis and needs. What the program aims to do is to give students a good grasp of Chinese radicals and stroke order rules, as well as to help students understand and appreciate the characteristics and formation of Chinese characters. The program includes writing practice on frequently used characters. Understanding the semantic function radicals have in the characters they form and having the ability to see compound characters by their simpler constituents enable students to memorize new characters in a logical way.

Using the CD-ROM as an Instructional Aid

The following diagram shows how a teacher might use the CD-ROM as an instructional aid to improve traditional classroom instruction.

	Textbook	*Multimedia CD-ROM*
Segment 1 (1st class hour)	**WARM-UP** Arouse students' interest and set the tone for the whole lesson	
	Get Started—Additional topic-related words to expand students' vocabulary for daily conversation	Text > Chant
Segment 2 (2nd class hour)	**Let's CHANT** Rhyming text to be read aloud	Drill > Word Builder Drill > Sentence Builder
Segment 3 (3rd class hour)	**Let's Learn GRAMMAR** Grammar	Text > Sentence Pattern Exercise > Word Game
Segment 4 (4th class hour)	**Let's TALK**	
	Scripted dialogue practice that may be extended or modified	Text > Dialogue
Segment 5 (5th class hour)	**Let's Learn PHRASE** **Let's Learn CHARACTER** **Let's Learn MEASURE WORD** **Let's Learn PUNCTUATION** Learn about Chinese characters, phrases, measure words, and punctuation	Exercise > Sentence Quiz #
	Let's READ Reading and comprehension	Text > Reading
Segment 6 (6th class hour)	**Let's DO IT** Review and reinforcement activities	
	LEARNING LOG Conclusion and students' self-evaluation	

#Sentence Quiz Exercise

The section *Exercise > Sentence Quiz* in the CD-ROM enhances learning by stimulating multiple senses as well as providing immediate feedback on students' performance.

The Sentence Quiz exercise comprises four levels.

- Level 1 – Warm-up Quiz (Look, Listen, and Type): Chinese text, *pinyin*, and audio prompts are provided.
- Level 2 – Visual-aid Quiz: Only Chinese text is provided. There are no *pinyin* or audio prompts.
- Level 3 – Audio-aid Quiz: Only audio prompts are provided.
- Level 4 – Character-selection Quiz: Only Chinese text is provided. After entering the correct *pinyin*, students are required to select the correct character from a list of similar-looking characters.

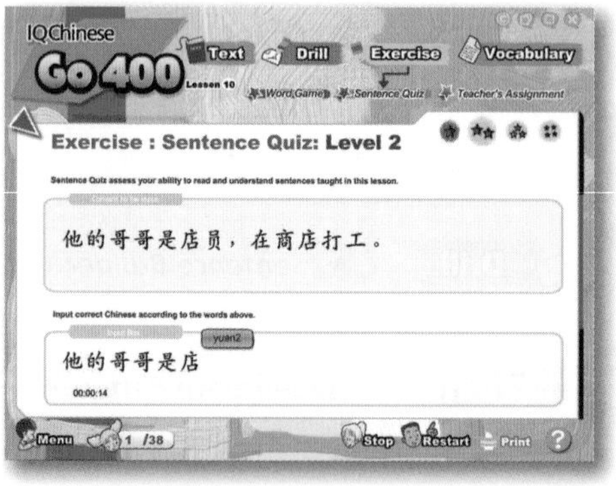

Typing practice for important sentences in every lesson reinforces the connection between words and sounds, and helps students to identify words better.

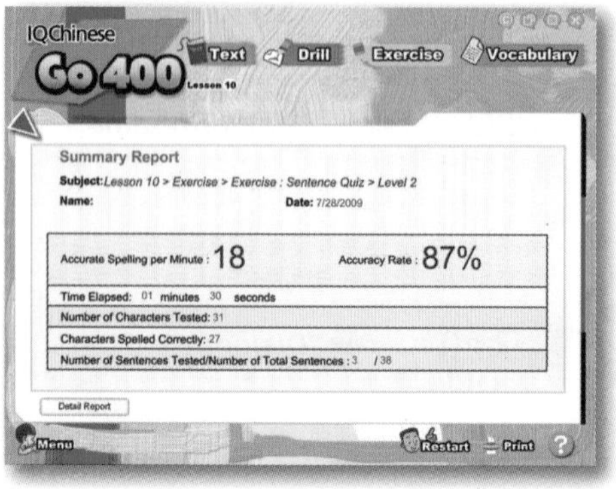

Summary Report immediately reveals students' accuracy rate and speed of typing per minute.

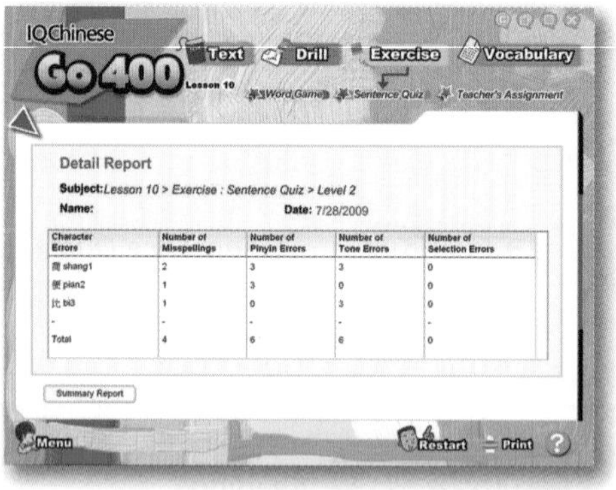

Detail Report lists characters typed erroneously three times during the quiz. It also shows details of errors based on categories such as *pinyin*, tone, and word selection. The instant feedback feature enables students to start on self-improvement right away.

Classroom Setup and Equipment

For small classes (up to 5 students), the teacher can show the CD-ROM features on one computer with students gathered around the screen. For large groups, a projector will be needed to project the computer's display onto a large screen so that the entire class can see.

If the classroom is not equipped with computers, the teacher may have students bring their own portable computers to class so that they can work individually or in small groups of 2 to 3 on the CD-ROM activities during designated class hours. CD-ROM activities may also be assigned as homework.

Suggestions for Teachers

We recommend that teachers

- spend 4-5 hours on each lesson in the Textbook and 2 hours on each lesson in the CD-ROM. The course materials and lesson length may be adjusted according to students' proficiency level and learning ability.
- allocate 1-2 class hours to go over with students the Review units in the Workbook as a way to check on the students' progress.
- have students complete 1-2 pages of the Workbook after every two class sessions.
- encourage students to spend 10 minutes a day on the Sentence Quiz in the CD-ROM. Practice makes perfect!

For detailed chapter-by-chapter lesson plans, teaching slides, and supplementary assignments, please refer to one of the following websites:

Cengage Learning http://www.cengageasia.com

IQChinese http://www.iqchinese.com

Scope & Sequence

Lesson	Communicative Goals	Vocabulary	Language Usage	Cultural Information
我的学校 My School 1	• Be able to talk about my school and its surroundings • Be able to describe the location of buildings and classrooms in relation to one another	**Description of my school** 教室, 办公室, 校长室, 体育馆, 运动场, 餐厅, 厕所, 楼上, 楼下, 楼, 知道, 旁边, 大楼, 校长, 上楼, 下楼…	• **Sentence pattern "知道……吗？"** 你知道谁在家吗？ • **Usage of "……边" and "……面" to indicate the position of an entity** 办公室在教室旁边。 图书馆在体育馆后面。 • **Difference in meaning when characters are transposed in a phrase ("楼上/楼下", "上楼/下楼")** 校长室在楼上，老师办公室在楼下。 你和我一起上楼。	• Levels of a building may be numbered differently in different countries.
我的学科 My Subjects 2	• Be able to talk about my subjects and my learning progress • Be able to use "什么都……" to sum up a group of similar items • Be able to use negative tags "没" and "不" appropriately • Be able to use "Adj + 地 + verb" to describe an action	**Academic subjects and learning** 数学, 科学, 历史, 地理, 体育, 美劳, 美术, 音乐, 史地, 科, 认真, 学科, 新, 错, 不错, 练习, 地(de), 认识, 难, 容易, 开始…	• **Sentence pattern "……，什么……都……"** 今天有电影、卡通和球赛，什么节目我都想看。 • **Usage of "错 / 不错 / 还不错"** 你走错路了。 你的中文写得不错。 A：这家饭馆的菜好吃吗？ B：还不错，下次我们一起去吃。 • **Usage of "的 / 得 / 地"** 这是我的教室。 我的数学小考考得不错。 妹妹和我一起开心地跳舞。 • **Usage of negative tag "不" and "没"** A：我做错了吗？ B：你没错。 他的成绩不错。	• Differences in the emphasis of school subjects between schools in America and Europe and in Asia
过生日 Celebrating Birthdays 3	• Be able to offer my friends birthday wishes • use "更" to express adjectives in varying degrees	**Birthday celebrations and well wishes** 祝, 生日, 快乐, 身体, 健康, 长(zhǎng), 过生日, 礼物, 祝福, 希望, 更, 庆祝, 帮, 帮忙…	• **Usage of adverb "更"** 他很高。 他哥哥更高。 • **Usage of "庆祝"** 今年你会在哪里庆祝生日？ • **Usage of "希望" in a sentence** 希望明天会更好。 • **Usage of "过"** 今年你会在哪里过生日？ 今年你会去外婆家过年吗？ • **Words that function as nouns as well as verbs** 祝福你天天快乐。 谢谢大家的祝福。	• Proper etiquette of handling birthday gifts in the Chinese culture • Birthday celebration for elderly relatives in the Chinese culture

Lesson	Communicative Goals	Vocabulary	Language Usage	Cultural Information
养小动物 Keeping Pets **4**	• Be able to name some common pets • Be able to describe what is needed to take care of small animals	**Responsibilities of keeping a pet** 动物, 狗, 猫, 鸟, 鱼, 养, 喂, 清理, 动物园, 公园, 它们, 大小便, 可爱, 只, 条...	• **Sentence pattern "带……去……"** 我带狗去散步。 • **Sentence pattern "是谁…… 的？"** 是谁带狗去散步的？ • **Expansion of sentences** 哥哥在家里养鱼。 哥哥在家里养了很多鱼。 哥哥在家里养了很多不同的鱼。	• The Chinese Zodiac • The functions of animals in traditional Chinese societies • The evolution of some Chinese characters from primitive illustrations of animals
我的假期 My Vacation **5**	• Be able to name various school or public holidays • Be able to describe my travel plans and to share my vacation experiences • Be able to express an inability to complete a task due to certain constraints	**Holidays and ways to spend a holiday** 假期, 春假, 暑假, 打工, 寒假, 旅行, 亲友, 周末, 放 (假), 别, 累, 别人, 别的, 只有, 假, 行...	• **Usage of "别"** 电视好看，可是别看太久。 这是别人的狗，不是我的狗。 别的学校都有体育馆，可是我的学校没有。 • **Usage of "只有"** 只有他会开车。 • **Sentence pattern "只有……，不够……的"** 我只有两天假，不够去旅行的。 • **Characters with different meanings in different words and phrases** 打：打字, 打架, 打电话, 打球, 打工 开：开心, 开车, 打开 长：校长, 长大, 长高, 长假期, 长桌子	• The different meanings of "打工" in different areas • In China, the New Year holiday falls around the Lunar New Year, typically around January or February.
我家房间 Rooms in My Home **6**	• Be able to name the different rooms in my home • Be able to state the functions of different rooms • Be able to indicate the completion of an action	**Different rooms and their functions** 房间, 客厅, 饭厅, 厨房, 睡房, 书房, 客房, 浴室, 客人, 坐, 洗澡, 上床, 睡觉, 东西, 东边, 西边, 经过, 请进, 间...	• **Sentence pattern "Verb + 过"** 弟弟洗过澡了。 • **Usage of "经过"** 从这里到办公室，你会经过我的教室。 • **Repetition of measure words** 一步一步 一课一课 • **Characters which have different meanings when they stand independently and when they are part of a word or phrase** 东、西、东西	• *Feng Shui*, the Chinese system for deciding the right position for a building and for organizing furniture or other objects in a house or a building
我用筷子 Using Chopsticks **7**	• Be able to identify the tableware and other features of Chinese and Western dining • Be able to use "把……" to describe the action imposed on an object and the result of that action on the object • Be able to use appropriate measure words on various items of tableware	**Chinese and Western tableware** 筷子, 汤匙, 汤勺, 刀子, 叉子, 碗, 盘子, 汤, 中餐, 西餐, 口, 慢, 把, 放...	• **Usage of "把"** 我喝完汤了。 → 我把汤喝完了。 • **Sentence pattern "……都可以，(subject) 都……"** 中餐、西餐都可以，我都喜欢。 • **Usage of "好"** 那本书好贵。 • **Measure words used on tableware** 碗, 盘, 双, 个, 把	• The origin of chopsticks and the etiquette of using chopsticks • The right way to hold chopsticks

Lesson	Communicative Goals	Vocabulary	Language Usage	Cultural Information
怎么去? How Do I Go? 8	• Be able to state the mode of transportation one would like to use to travel to one's destination • Be able to express the sequence of two events • Be able to use "才" to state that a result can only be achieved under certain conditions	**Traveling by public transportation** 汽车, 出租车, 计程车, 公交车, 公车, 地铁, 飞机, 赶得上, 搭, 赶, 交通, 先, 机场, 才, 快, 车站, 转车...	• **Sentence pattern "先……再……"** 大家要先洗手再吃饭。 • **Usage of "才"** 早上车多，上学要坐地铁才快。 • **Verb phrase "Verb 来 Verb 去"** 走→走来走去	• The evolution of some Chinese characters from primitive illustrations of transportation
我们的大地 The Earth 9	• Be able to describe if our environment is clean and state ways to preserve our environment • Become familiar with the use of ordinal numbers • Be able to use "只有……，才……" to indicate that a result can only be achieved under the stated conditions	**Cleanliness of our environment and ways to preserve it** 干净, 脏, 安静, 吵, 舒服, 大地, 安全, 脏乱, 第, 注意, 第……名, 乱丢, 意思, 乱...	• **Usage of "第 + Numeral + (Measure Word)"** 过马路要注意车子，安全第一。这是我第一次自己坐飞机，很紧张。 • **Usage of "Verb + 着"** 书上写着：大地是你我的家。 • **Sentence pattern "只有……，才……"** 只有多练习，才容易学会。 • **Sentence pattern "只要……，就……"** 只要多练习，就容易学会。 • **Word classes** noun, verb, adjective	• China's top protected species: The Giant Panda
工作天地 Work and Occupations 10	• Be able to talk about my ambition, and display a good work attitude • Be able to use "或" to offer a choice between two alternatives	**Occupations and attitudes toward work** 工作, 天地, 演员, 警员, 运动员, 店员, 医师, 律师, 工程师, 职业, 兴趣, 一直, 或, 需要...	• **Usage of "一直"** 舅舅一直找不到工作。 • **Usage of "或"** 星期五或星期六我都可以去看电影。 • **Usage of "需要"** 我需要电脑才能做今天的功课。 • **Rewriting sentences by changing the structure** 太累的工作，他不想要。 →他不想要太累的工作。 • **Usage of Chinese punctuation "、" (pause mark)** 工程师、演员和工人，每一种职业都很重要。	• The origin of the names of some occupations such as teacher (老师), lawyer (律师), and engineer (工程师).

Table of Contents

LESSON 1

我的学校
My School

My Goals

1 Be able to talk about my school and its surroundings
2 Be able to describe the location of the buildings and classrooms in my school in relation to one another
3 Be able to recognize how the order of Chinese characters in a word determines its meaning
4 Become familiar with vocabulary associated with classrooms, schools, and their facilities

Get Started

jiào shì
教室

bàn gōng shì
办公室

xiào zhǎng shì
校长室

图书馆

tǐ yù guǎn
体育馆

yùn dòng chǎng
运动场

lóu shàng lóu xià
楼上/楼下
(upstairs) (downstairs)

cān tīng
餐厅

cè suǒ
厕所

Show and Tell

1 Take photographs of the above areas in your school.
2 Create a slideshow with the photographs and present to your class the areas you walk by every day.

New Words

jiào shì 教室 classroom
bàn gōng shì 办公室 office
xiào zhǎng shì 校长室 principal's office
tǐ yù guǎn 体育馆 gym
yùn dòng chǎng 运动场 stadium
cān tīng 餐厅 dining hall, cafeteria
cè suǒ 厕所 restroom

Let's CHANT

Go400

学校里有图书馆，

jiào shì cān tīng tǐ yù guǎn

教室餐厅体育馆，

lóu shàng lóu xià cè suǒ

楼上楼下有厕所，

lóu bàn gōng shì

一楼还有办公室。

TIP In some places such as China and the United States, the ground level is known as the first story. In other places such as Britain, the first story is the first level above the ground level. When traveling, one should be sure of how the levels of a building are numbered in that country to avoid getting lost.

(In the U.S.)

(In Britain)

New Words

lóu shàng
楼上 upstairs

lóu xià
楼下 downstairs

lóu
楼 story; floor

Let's Learn GRAMMAR

zhī dào
知道……吗？

zhī dào
你知道谁在家吗？

zhī dào
他知道怎么去吗？

zhī dào cè suǒ
你知道厕所在哪里吗？

zhī dào
爸爸知道这台电脑多少钱吗？

zhī dào
小明知道哪里有医院吗？

TIP Although these sentences already contain interrogative markers such as "谁" and "怎么", the question tag "吗" is still required at the end of the sentences. This is because "吗" is often paired up with "知道" to form Yes/No questions. The answers to "谁在家" and "怎么去" are what the speaker would like to know, and hence they are placed after the verb "知道".

zhī dào
你知道妈妈要买什么吗？

zhī dào
我知道，妈妈要买笔和书给我们。

New Words

zhī dào
知道 know

preposition of location	上	下	左	右	前	后	páng 旁
边	上边	下边	左边	右边	前边	后边	páng biān 旁边
面	上面	下面	左面	右面	前面	后面	–

bàn gōng shì jiào shì páng biān
办公室在教室旁边。

tǐ yù guǎn
图书馆在体育馆后面。

New Words

páng biān
旁边 beside, next to

我在这一边，小明在那一边。

cè suǒ cè suǒ
女厕所在这一边，男厕所在那一边。

Go400

WANT TO LEARN MORE?

Check out the Text > Sentence Pattern section in the Go400 CD.

Let's TALK

Find a partner and practice the following dialogues.

Task 1

zhī dào cè suǒ
A: 请问你知道厕所在哪里吗？

lóu cè suǒ cè suǒ lóu
B: 二楼没有厕所，厕所在一楼。

A: 谢谢！

cè suǒ cè suǒ
B: 女厕所在左边，男厕所在右边。

zhī dào
A: 好！我知道了。

Task 2

bàn gōng shì
A: 请问老师办公室在哪里？

tǐ yù guǎn páng biān dà lóu
B: 就在体育馆旁边的大楼里。

bàn gōng shì lóu
A: 你知道老师办公室在几楼吗？

lóu
B: 在三楼。

TIP

In the United States, secondary school students can choose a combination of their preferred subjects. Before class, students may visit the library or gym in their own time before proceeding to various classrooms for different subjects. In other countries such as China, all students in a class study the same subjects, so each class remains in a pre-allocated classroom while the teachers move between classrooms. Students only travel to special classrooms when a lesson requires such a need.

New Words

dà lóu
大楼 building

Task 3

zhī dào xiào zhǎng shì
A: 你知道校长室在哪里吗？

dà lóu lóu
B: 在前面大楼的二楼。

bàn gōng shì
A: 老师办公室也在那里吗？

xiào zhǎng shì páng biān bàn gōng shì
B: 校长室旁边就是老师办公室。

zhī dào
A: 我知道了，谢谢！

Task 4

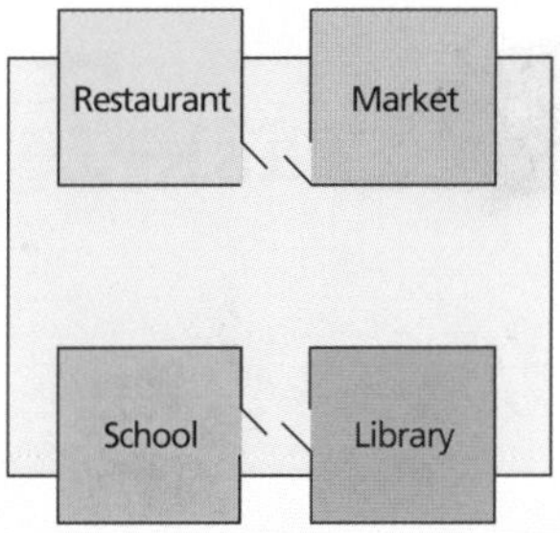

zhī dào
A: 你知道从图书馆到市场怎么走吗？

B: ________________________________。

zhī dào
A: 你知道妈妈要买什么吗？

B: ________________________________。

zhī dào lóu
A: 你知道买牛奶要去几楼吗？

B: ________________________________。

The following dialogues are adapted from the Text > Dialogue section in your Go400. Listen to the CD before reading the transcript on this page.

Task 5

A: 你的教室(jiào shì)在哪里？

B: 在左边的大楼(dà lóu)里。

Task 6

A: 你知道(zhī dào)他的电话吗？

B: 对不起，我不知道(zhī dào)。

Task 7

A: 请问你找哪一位？

B: 我找校长(xiào zhǎng)。你知道(zhī dào)他在哪里吗？

Task 8

A: 我们去哪里吃饭？

B: 附近有一家中国餐厅(cān tīng)，便宜又好吃，停车也方便。

Extend Dialogues

1 Choose two dialogues from Tasks 5 to 8.

2 Combine the two dialogues into one. Add three more exchanges to the dialogue to extend it to 10 sentences.

3 Upon completion, record your dialogue and ask your teacher for comments.

New Words

xiào zhǎng
校长 principal

Let's Learn PHRASE

In Chinese morphology, two characters are commonly combined to create a word. The order in which the two characters appear determines the meaning of the word. Can you differentiate between the following words?

lóu shàng lóu xià
楼上/楼下

xiào zhǎng shì lóu shàng bàn gōng shì lóu xià
校长室在楼上，老师办公室在楼下。

lóu shàng xiào zhǎng lóu xià
我去楼上找校长，你在楼下等我。

shàng lóu xià lóu
上楼/下楼

shàng lóu
你和我一起上楼。

xià lóu
奶奶，你下楼要小心。

New Words

shàng lóu
上楼 (go) up the stairs

xià lóu
下楼 (go) down the stairs

lóu shàng
小明在楼上，我要去找他。

shàng lóu lóu xià
好，你上楼找小明，我在楼下等你。

Let's READ

Text 1 Go400

Read the following text carefully.

我们的学校不大，可是什么都有：一楼(lóu)有校长(xiào zhǎng)室(shì)、办公室(bàn gōng shì)、老师休息室(xiū xí shì)*，还有体育馆(tǐ yù guǎn)、图书馆、餐厅(cān tīng)和厕所(cè suǒ)；二楼(lóu)和三楼(lóu)有很多教室(jiào shì)。大楼(dà lóu)的旁边(páng biān)是运动场(yùn dòng chǎng)，我们可以打球，可以跑步。

我们的学校不大，可是什么都有。最重要的是，我们有好校长(xiào zhǎng)、好老师，还有好同学。大家都爱我们的学校。

*老师休息室 staff lounge

Answer these questions in Chinese.

1 Where are the classrooms in the author's school located? Where is the stadium located?

2 According to the author's description, which of the following sentences is <u>true</u>?

- ☐ 作者(zuò zhě)(author)的学校很大。
- ☐ 作者喜欢自己的学校。
- ☐ 作者的学校，什么老师都有。

3 What does the author find about his school that is more important than the facilities?

Want More Practice?

Write an essay about your school. Type it out into a report.

Go400 WANT TO LEARN MORE?

Check out the Text > Reading section in the Go400 CD.

Text 2

Read the following text carefully.

xīn

九月了，我到新*学校去上学。

xīn gōng yuán xīn

新学校有很多树，就和公园*一样。新学校里没有

tǐ yù guǎn yùn dòng chǎng gāo lóu

体育馆，可是有一个很大的运动场。那里没有高楼*，

bàn gōng shì jiào shì lóu

办公室和教室都在一楼。

xiào zhǎng shì bàn gōng shì xiào zhǎng shì

校长室右边是图书馆，老师办公室在校长室左边。

bàn gōng shì páng biān jiào shì cè suǒ jiào shì

老师办公室旁边就是我们的中文教室。男厕所在教室

cè suǒ

这一边，女厕所在图书馆那一边。

cān tīng

我和同学每天一起去餐厅吃饭，也常常去图书馆

看书。我们一起上学，一起回家。

*新 new *公园 park
*高楼 high-rise building

Answer these questions in Chinese.

1 What facilities are there in the author's school? Check the appropriate boxes below.
☐公园 ☐体育馆 ☐图书馆 ☐办公室 ☐厕所 ☐高楼

2 What activities does the author share with his school mates?

3 Fill in the blanks below with "图书馆", "校长室", "老师办公室", and "中文教室" according to their location in relation to one another as mentioned in the text.

← Left Right →

Let's DO IT

1 Split the class into three or four teams.

2 As a team, fill in the floor plan below with the areas from page 2 in any order. Write three sentences describing your classroom's location in relation to the areas you have chosen.

3 Each team will take turns to read out the three descriptions.

4 The other teams must try to figure out the floor plan. Guessing teams take turns to ask Yes / No questions such as "男厕所(cè suǒ)旁边(páng biān)是教室(jiào shì)吗？". The host team may refute or affirm the question such as "对，男厕所(cè suǒ)旁边(páng biān)是教室(jiào shì)。", or "不对，男厕所(cè suǒ)旁边(páng biān)不是教室(jiào shì)。".

5 The first team which draws the complete floor plan wins.

FLOOR PLAN

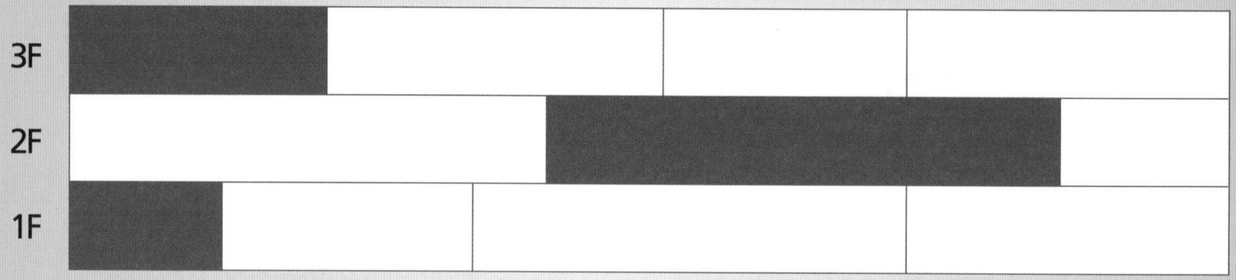

SENTENCES

1

2

3

LEARNING LOG

I can...	Excellent	Good	Fair	Needs Improvement
1 name the buildings and classrooms in my school.	☐	☐	☐	☐
2 describe the location of the buildings and classrooms in my school.	☐	☐	☐	☐
3 use the sentence structure "知道……吗？" to ask questions.	☐	☐	☐	☐
4 rearrange the order of "楼上" and "楼下" to convey different meanings.	☐	☐	☐	☐
5 write "知", "道", "办", "楼", and "室".	☐	☐	☐	☐

LESSON

2

我的学科

My Subjects

PERIOD	Semester 1	Semester 2
	DAY A	
1	Physical Education	Physical Education
2	History	History
5	Interior Design	Art
7	Human Biology	Human Biology
	DAY B	
2	Advanced English	Advanced English
4	Symphony Orchestra	Symphony Orchestra
6	World Civilizations	Film History & Appreciation
8	Pre-Calculus	Pre-Calculus

My Goals

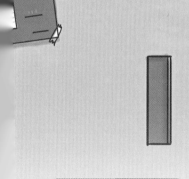

1. Be able to talk about the subjects that I study
2. Be able to sum up a group of similar items
3. Be able to differentiate between negative tag "没" and "不", and use them appropriately
4. Become familiar with the vocabulary associated with subjects taught in school

Get Started

学校课外活动多，
参加乐队还打球，
下课回家想休息，
可是还得做功课。

中文

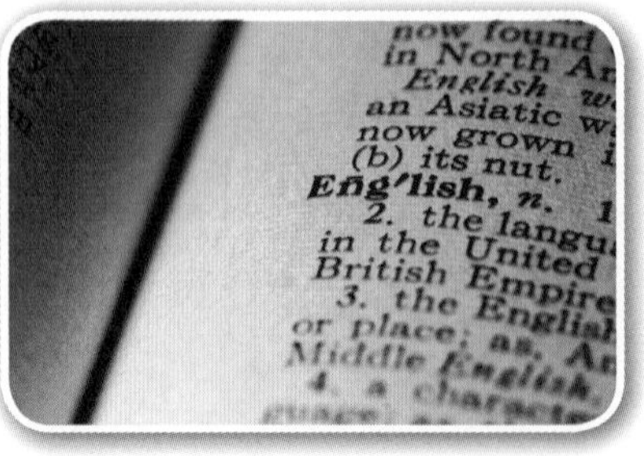

英文

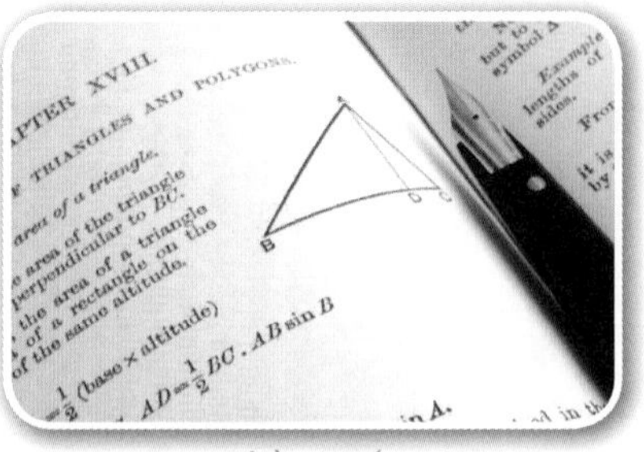

shù xué
数学

kē xué
科学

lì shǐ
历史

dì lǐ
地理

tǐ yù
体育

měi láo měi shù
美劳/美术

yīn yuè
音乐

New Words

xué kē 学科 subject	shù xué 数学 Mathematics	kē xué 科学 Science	lì shǐ 历史 History
dì lǐ 地理 Geography	tǐ yù 体育 Physical Education	měi láo měi shù 美劳/美术 Art	yīn yuè 音乐 Music

Introduce It

Tell your classmates about your favorite subject — why you like it, when the class takes place, etc.

Let's CHANT

Go 400

shù xué
数学英文每天有，

kē xué shǐ dì
还有科学和史地，

tǐ yù yīn yuè měi láo
体育音乐加美劳，

kē rèn zhēn
每科都要认真学。

Talk About It

1 Use the Internet to research on the typical timetable of a secondary school student in other countries. Alternatively, if you have friends studying overseas, compare your timetable with theirs. What are the similarities and differences?

2 In Asia, schools tend to emphasize more on academic subjects such as languages and Mathematics. In Europe and America, schools tend to focus more on physical education and extra-curricular activities. What subject do you think is most important? Why?

New Words

shǐ dì
史地 History and Geography

kē
科 subject

rèn zhēn
认真 take seriously

Let's Learn GRAMMAR

今天有电影、卡通和球赛，什么节目我都想看。

In this instance, "什么" has no specific referent. Placed before "都" and "也", it encompasses all of the subjects mentioned before it.

学校有英文、中文、数学(shù xué)和体育(tǐ yù)，什么课我都想学。

我有很多鞋，有白鞋、红鞋和黑鞋，什么颜色(yán sè) (color)的鞋我都喜欢。

学校里的活动，什么都有趣(yǒu qù) (interesting)。

这家餐厅，什么都好吃。

早餐有牛奶、面包和果汁，什么都好吃。

教室里有新(xīn)桌子、新(xīn)椅子和新黑板(xīn hēi bǎn) (blackboard)，什么都是新(xīn)的。

New Words

新(xīn) new

Go400

WANT TO LEARN MORE?

Check out the Text > Sentence Pattern section in the Go400 CD.

错/不错/还不错

cuò bú cuò bú cuò

你走错路了。

这个问题你答错了。

你的中文写得不错。

他常常练习跑步，所以体育成绩很不错。

A：那家饭馆的菜好吃吗？

B：还不错，下次我们一起去吃。

的/得/地

TIP

"的" is commonly used with adjectives and nouns. "Noun + 的 + noun" shows possession, e.g. 妈妈的衣服. "Adjective + 的 + noun" expresses a noun phrase where the adjective describes the noun, e.g. 漂亮的衣服.

"得" commonly appears after a verb. It functions as an adverbial to describe the action in greater detail.

"地" typically precedes a verb. "Adjective + 地" is added before a verb as an adverbial to describe the action in greater detail.

这是我的教室。

他是认真的学生。

我的数学小考考得不错。

我常常和堂哥比赛，看谁跑得快(quickly)。

妹妹和我一起开心地跳舞。

下个星期就要比赛了，我要认真地练习。

New Words

错 cuò wrong	不错 bú cuò not bad; good	练习 liàn xí practice	地 de (a particle used after an adverbial)

Let's TALK

Find partner(s) and practice the following dialogues.

Task 1

rèn shi
A: 你认识王老师吗？

yīn yuè
B: 她是教音乐的吗？

A: 对！

rèn shi
B: 我认识她，你要找她吗？

A: 是的。请问她的办公室在哪里？

B: 在左边大楼的二楼。

Task 2

A: 我一个星期要上很多课，每天都有
shù xué
数学课，每个星期还要上两次中文课。

kē nán kē róng yì
B: 哪一科最难？哪一科最容易？

nán shù xué róng yì shù xué bú cuò
A: 英文最难，数学最容易，我的数学成绩很不错。

xué kē
B: 你最喜欢什么学科？

xué kē
A: 我什么学科都喜欢。

New Words

rèn shi
认识 know

nán
难 difficult

róng yì
容易 easy

Task 3

New Words

开始 (kāi shǐ) start, begin

A: 中文好学吗？

B: 一开始(kāi shǐ)好学，现在就不好学了。

A: 为什么？

B: 因为中文字又多又难(nán)写，很容易(róng yì)忘。

A: 多练习(liàn xí)就不会忘。你可以和我一样，一边打字，一边听声音(shēng yīn) (sound)。常常练习(liàn xí)，很容易(róng yì)就学会了。

Task 4

A: 上午我要上数学(shù xué)课和英文课。你们要上什么课？

B: 我有科学(kē xué)课和美劳(měi láo)课。

C: 我有史地(shǐ dì)课和音乐(yīn yuè)课。

A: 上午大家上的课都不一样，可是下午我们都有体育(tǐ yù)课。

The following dialogues are adapted from the Text > Dialogue section in your Go 400. Listen to the CD before reading the transcript on this page.

Task 5

kāi shǐ
A: 我们什么时候开始上课？

B: 八点半。

Task 6

rèn shi
A: 你认识他吗？

rèn shi
B: 我认识他，他叫谢小明，是我的同学。

Task 7

A: 这(一)家餐厅的菜好吃吗？

bú cuò
B: 还不错，可是很贵。

The numeral "一" may be omitted in the sentence structure "这 / 那 + 一 + measure word + noun".

Task 8

róng yì
A: 学中文容易吗？

róng yì　　　liàn xí
B: 不容易，要常常练习。

Want More Practice?

Rewrite the dialogues in Tasks 6 to 8, changing B's answers to the opposite of the original answers. Find a partner to practice reading the new dialogues.

Let's Learn PHRASE

Though both "不" and "没" are negative markers, they are not used interchangeably. "不" is used to negate current or future action or situation while "没" is only used to negate a past action or situation. Some verbs such as "是", "知道", and "可以" can only be modified by "不" while other verbs like "有" can only be modified by "没". With such differences in their meanings, "不" and "没" should not be confused. Can you identify the differences between the negative markers in the examples below?

你的中文说得不错(bú cuò)。

他的成绩还不错(bú cuò)。

TIP "错" means "incorrect"; however, "不错" does not mean "correct" with the addition of the negative marker "不". Instead, it means "not bad; good".

你说得没错(cuò)，和同学打架是不对的。

A: 我做错(cuò)了吗？

B: 你没错(cuò)，你做得很好。

TIP There are different usages for "还" in this book. First, it conveys "fairly" or "passably" in a reluctant tone, like "还不错" and "还可以". Next, it denotes further elaboration or an increase in extent or quantity, such as "会认字，还要会写字". Another expresses an outcome of a comparison, indicating a situation still remains unchanged, such as "我还是不知道车站在哪里".

Practice It

Fill in the blanks with "不" or "没".

1. ☐错！他就是我的音乐老师。
2. 学中文☐容易，可是我的中文成绩还☐错。
3. 我☐知道餐厅在哪里。
4. 那个人☐是我弟弟，我☐有弟弟。
5. 我的功课还☐做完，我☐能出去玩。

Let's READ

Text 1

Go400

Read the following text carefully.

kāi xué　xīn　xīn　xīn
　　九月，开学*了，什么都是新的：新的学校、新
xīn　xīn　xīn　xīn　kè
的教室、新的老师和新的同学；新的书包、新的课
běn　xīn　běn zi
本*，还有新的本子*。

xué qī　xīn
　　这个学期*，大家有很多新的课：上午，有的人
shù xué　kē xué　shǐ dì
有数学课和英文课，有的人有科学科和史地课；下
tǐ yù　měi láo
午，有的人要上体育课，有的人要上美劳课。除了
上课，我还要参加很多课外活动。

xīn　xué qī　kāi shǐ　rèn zhēn de
　　新的学期，新的开始，我会认真地学。

*开学 beginning of a new semester *课本 textbook
*本子 notebook *学期 semester

Answer these questions in Chinese.

1 What is new for the author in the new semester?

2 Apart from his classes, what other activities does the author participate in?

3 What do you think the author means when he says "什么都是新的"?

Text 2

Read the following text carefully.

妹妹说，学中文不容易(róng yì)。弟弟说，学英文不容易(róng yì)。

妈妈问，为什么不容易(róng yì)？

妹妹说，中文字很难(nán)写，有的字笔画(bǐ huà)*很多。弟弟说，英文字很多，要认识(rèn shi)很多字才(cái)*能看新闻。

妈妈听了，对他们说："你们说得都没错，每一种语言(yǔ yán)*，一开始(kāi shǐ)学的时候都很难(nán)，要说出字的读音(dú yīn)*，要认识(rèn shi)字的意思(yì si)*，还要会写字。可是多练习(liàn xí)，认真(rèn zhēn)学，很快就学会了。"

*笔画 stroke　*才 just　*语言 language　*读音 pronunciation　*意思 meaning

Answer these questions in Chinese.

1 Why does the author's younger sister find it tough to learn Chinese?
2 The author's younger brother finds it tough to learn English too. Is his reason the same as his sister's?
3 Who does their mother agree with? Why?
4 Do you know a good method to learn a language? Share it with your classmates.

Go400

WANT TO LEARN MORE?

Check out the Text > Reading section in the Go400 CD.

Let's DO IT

1 Using a computer, create your timetable. Bring the timetable to class and answer the following questions.

❶ 你今年选了几个学科(xué kē)？有哪些学科(xué kē)？

❷ 你最喜欢哪一科(kē)？你最不喜欢哪一科(kē)？为什么？

❸ 哪一科(kē)最容易(róng yì)、最难(nán)、最有用？(Fill in the table below.)

	喜欢	不喜欢	容易 (róng yì)	难 (nán)	有用
学科 (xué kē)					

2 Each student is to place his timetable in a box. Assign a representative to randomly draw the timetables out one by one to form teams of three.

3 In the team of three, share your answers to the above questions, and find out similarities and differences among the three timetables. You may either write your findings down or record them using a recording device.

LEARNING LOG

I can...	Excellent	Good	Fair	Needs Improvement
1 talk about the subjects that I study.	☐	☐	☐	☐
2 use "什么" to sum up a host of similar items.	☐	☐	☐	☐
3 use "的", "得", and "地" appropriately.	☐	☐	☐	☐
4 differentiate between the meanings of "错", "不错", and "还不错".	☐	☐	☐	☐
5 write "认", "识", "练", "习", and "错".	☐	☐	☐	☐

LESSON

3 过生日
Celebrating Birthdays

My Goals

1 Be able to offer my friends birthday wishes
2 Be able to express adjectives in varying degrees
3 Be able to recognize words that may function as verbs and nouns
4 Become familiar with words associated with well-wishes and blessings

Get Started

zhù shēng rì kuài lè
祝你生日快乐！

zhù shēn tǐ jiàn kāng
祝你身体健康！

zhù
祝你天天开心！

zhù kuài lè
祝你幸福快乐！

zhù zhǎng
祝你长得又高又大！

zhù
祝你一年比一年好！

TIP Can you sing "Happy Birthday" in Chinese? Try it out with the lyrics below. You might find it useful the next time you attend a friend's birthday party!

‖ 5 5 6 5 1 7 – |
祝 你 生 日 快 乐！

| 5 5 6 5 2 1 – |
祝 你 生 日 快 乐！

| 5 5 3 2 1 7 6 |
祝 你 生 日 快 乐！

| 4 4 3 1 2 1 – ‖
祝 你 生 日 快 乐！

New Words

zhù
祝 wish

shēng rì
生日 birthday

kuài lè
快乐 happy

shēn tǐ
身体 body

jiàn kāng
健康 healthy

zhǎng
长 grow

Let's CHANT

Go 400

guò shēng rì　　kuài lè
过生日，真快乐，

　　　　　　lǐ wù
朋友送你小礼物，

　　　　　　zhù fú
大家唱歌又祝福，

xī wàng　　　gèng
希望明年会更好。

TIP

When attending a party, you may have prepared a gift for the host. The host may also prepare party favors for his guests. In some countries, the host will open his presents immediately to show his appreciation. In China, however, it is proper etiquette to leave the gifts unopened until the guests have left.

New Words

guò shēng rì 过生日 celebrate one's birthday　lǐ wù 礼物 gift　zhù fú 祝福 wishes　xī wàng 希望 hope　gèng 更 more (+ adj.)

Let's Learn GRAMMAR

gèng
更

gèng
他很高。他哥哥更高。

gèng
我的成绩不错。他的成绩更好。

gèng kuài
哥哥每天练习跑步，现在他跑得更快(fast)了。

xī wàng zhǎng gèng
小明想参加篮球队，他希望明年能长得更高一点儿。

gèng
今天41°F，明天35°F，明天的天气会比今天更冷。

TIP

In a comparison, "更" is used before an adjective to express it in a greater degree as compared to before.

For example:

→ "我的成绩不错。他的成绩更好。" means "his results are better than mine".

→ "他希望明年能长得更高一点儿。" means "he wishes to be taller next year".

qìng zhù
庆祝

qìng zhù shēng rì
今年你会在哪里庆祝生日？

qìng zhù
比赛赢了，我们要庆祝。

shēng rì bāng qìng zhù
明天是外婆七十岁生日，我们要帮她庆祝。

New Words

qìng zhù
庆祝 celebrate

bāng
帮 help

Go400

WANT TO LEARN MORE?

Check out the Text > Sentence Pattern section in the Go400 CD.

xī wàng 希望

xī wàng gèng
希望明天会更好。

xī wàng bāng máng
希望你能来帮忙。

xī wàng shēn tǐ jiàn kāng
希望你身体健康。

xī wàng lǐ wù
希望你喜欢我送你的礼物。

xī wàng
希望明天的球赛我们会赢。

TIP "希望" here is used as a verb. By starting a sentence with "希望", the subject (the speaker) at the beginning of the sentence may be omitted.

New Words

bāng máng
帮忙 help

guò 过

guò shēng rì
今年你会在哪里过生日？

guò shēng rì lǐ wù
你过生日，爸爸会送礼物给你吗？

guò nián
今年你会去外婆家过年 (celebrate the New Year) 吗？

guò jié jié rì
我喜欢过节 (celebrate a festival)，不一样的节日 (festival)，

qìng zhù
有不一样的庆祝活动。

TIP Of its several meanings, "过" also means "庆祝" (celebrate). However, "过" is used more in speech and may be used in "过生日", "过节", "过年", and so on. In comparison with "庆祝", the meaning of "过" is more limited and it does not have the connotations that "庆祝" carry. It also sounds less formal.

Let's TALK

Find a partner and practice the following dialogues.

Task 1

zhù shēng rì kuài lè gèng
A: 小方，祝你生日快乐，明年更好！

shēng rì
B: 谢谢！你怎么知道今天是我的生日？

A: 我问了你哥哥，他说的。

shēng rì
B: 你的生日是几月几号？

A: 下个月五号。请你来我家，
guò shēng rì
和我一起过生日，好吗？

B: 好。

xī wàng
A: 我也找了小贵，希望他能一起来。

Task 2

A: 为什么你要练习唱歌？

shēng rì
B: 明天是我妈妈生日，我要唱歌给她听。

shēng rì
A: 我唱歌不好听，所以我不唱。妈妈生日那一
bāng jiā wù
天，我会帮她做家务(household chores)。

Task 3

A: 我爷爷八十岁了，明天我们要帮(bāng)他庆祝(qìng zhù)。

B: 你要送什么礼物(lǐ wù)给你爷爷？

A: 我用电脑做了一张卡片(kǎ piàn)(card)，祝(zhù)他健康(jiàn kāng)、快乐(kuài lè)。希望(xī wàng)爷爷喜欢我送他的礼物(lǐ wù)。

B: 这是很好的礼物(lǐ wù)，你爷爷一定(yí dìng)(certainly)喜欢。

TIP

Celebrating an Elderly Person's Birthday

In the past when life expectancy was shorter, people in China would hold elaborate celebrations (known as "大寿(dà shòu)") to mark a person's sixtieth birthday, and would continue to do so for every decade of his life thereafter. The birthday celebrations would typically involve lavish banquets to wish the person good health and longevity. During such festivities, the following foods were usually prepared because of their cultural significance:

寿桃 (shòu táo)

According to Chinese legends, when one eats peaches from the celestial skies, he would gain perpetual youth. Hence, peaches are known to mean longevity. However, the longevity peaches used in the birthday celebrations are actually made of flour, and are commonly filled in the center with red bean.

寿面 (shòu miàn)

The long strands of noodles symbolize longevity. It is believed that one would be blessed with long life if he eats such long strands of noodles. Since the noodles represent long life, one should not sever the noodles by biting them off; instead, he should take an entire mouthful and chew it in the mouth.

Task 4

Can you identify pairs of dialogue from the eight utterances below? Organize them into four dialogues and fill in the following table. When this is done, you may listen to the Text > Dialogue section in your Go400 for the correct answers.

1	A:	2	A:	3	A:	4	A:
	B:		B:		B:		B:

❶ 下个星期六，也就是三月十二号。

bāng qìng zhù

❷ 妈妈会在家里帮我庆祝，你可以来吗？

qìng zhù shēng rì

❸ 你会在哪里庆祝生日？

bāng máng bāng máng

❹ 没问题，我可以帮你忙。/对不起，我不能帮忙。

lǐ wù

❺ 谢谢你的礼物。

bāng máng

❻ 你可以帮我忙吗？

shēng rì

❼ 你的生日是哪一天？

zhù shēng rì kuài lè

❽ 祝你生日快乐！

Think and Answer

1 Which three utterances could be linked to form a meaningful dialogue?

2 Imagine Tom asks Susan to do him a favor by inviting Lily to a birthday party. Compose a dialogue comprising at least four utterances, of which one must be "你可以帮我忙吗？".

Let's Learn PHRASE

Some words may belong to more than one word class. For some words, their usage varies according to whether they function as a noun or a verb in the context. The boxes below show how these words "希望 (xī wàng)", "祝福 (zhù fú)", and "帮忙 (bāng máng)" are used differently.

Verb

xī wàng ... qìng zhù shēng rì
我希望可以和朋友一起庆祝生日。

xī wàng
爸爸希望我学好中文。

xī wàng
希望明天你可以来我家。

Noun

shēn tǐ jiàn kāng ... xī wàng
我们身体健康是妈妈最大的希望。

xī wàng
哥哥最大的希望是参加球队。

xī wàng ... kuài lè
一个人有希望就会快乐。

zhù fú ... kuài lè
祝福(V.)你天天快乐。

zhù fú
谢谢大家的祝福(N.)。

xī wàng ... bāng máng
希望(V.)你明天能来帮忙(V.)。

bāng máng ... gèng
有了你的帮忙(N.)，我的中文说得更好了。

V. = verb
N. = noun

Let's READ

Text 1

Read the following text carefully.

今天是姐姐二十岁生日。她穿上妈妈送她的新衣服，戴上爸爸送她的红帽子。大家唱生日歌，祝她生日快乐；大家祝福她，祝她这一年开心。她打开每一个礼物，她谢谢每一个家人。

姐姐说：“过生日真好！我要谢谢大家帮我庆祝，我还要谢谢爸爸妈妈给我二十年的爱。我祝福爸爸妈妈身体健康，我也祝福大家，一天比一天好，一年比一年好！”

Answer these questions in Chinese.

1 What did Older Sister wear for her birthday? Who were the gifts from?

2 Why did Older Sister thank her parents, as well as everybody else?

3 What birthday wishes did Older Sister receive? What did she wish for everybody in return?

Text 2

Read the following text carefully.

上个星期五是我十四岁生日(shēng rì)。

生日(shēng rì)那天，妈妈做了蛋糕(dàn gāo)*和好吃的菜，我请朋友来我家，和我一起过生日(guò shēng rì)。唱完“生日快乐(shēng rì kuài lè)”歌，大家送我生日礼物(shēng rì lǐ wù)，祝(zhù)我明年更(gèng)好。爷爷说我这一年上课很认真，他要送我一个大礼物(lǐ wù)，就是我最想要的电脑。

我要谢谢大家的祝福(zhù fú)，也希望(xī wàng)大家天天开心。

*蛋糕 cake

Answer these questions in Chinese.

1 What did the author do for his birthday?

2 What birthday wishes did the author receive? What did he wish for everybody in return?

3 Would you consider a computer big gift? Why do you think the author's grandfather says the computer is a big gift?

Go400 **WANT TO LEARN MORE?**

Check out the Text > Reading section in the Go400 CD.

Let's DO IT

Choose five classmates to work with. With the following questions, find out when their birthdays are, and what birthday presents they would like to receive. Finally, write down birthday wishes for each of them.

❶ 请问你的生(shēng)日(rì)是几月几日？

❷ 你想要什么生(shēng)日(rì)礼(lǐ)物(wù)？

❸ 我祝(zhù)福(fú)你"健(jiàn)康(kāng)快(kuài)乐(lè)"。

	Name	Birthday	Birthday present	Birthday wishes
1				
2				
3				
4				
5				

LEARNING LOG

I can...	Excellent	Good	Fair	Needs Improvement
1 offer my family or friends well wishes on their birthdays.	☐	☐	☐	☐
2 use "更 + adjective" to express the adjective in a stronger degree.	☐	☐	☐	☐
3 use "过" and "庆祝" appropriately in sentences.	☐	☐	☐	☐
4 use "希望", "祝福", and "帮忙" appropriately as verbs as well as nouns.	☐	☐	☐	☐
5 write "希", "望", "更", "健", and "康".	☐	☐	☐	☐

LESSON

4

养小动物
Keeping Pets

My Goals

1 Be able to name some common small animals
2 Be able to describe what is needed to take care of small animals
3 Understand how some Chinese characters evolved from illustrations
4 Become familiar with vocabulary associated with keeping pets

Get Started

gǒu
狗

māo
猫

niǎo
鸟

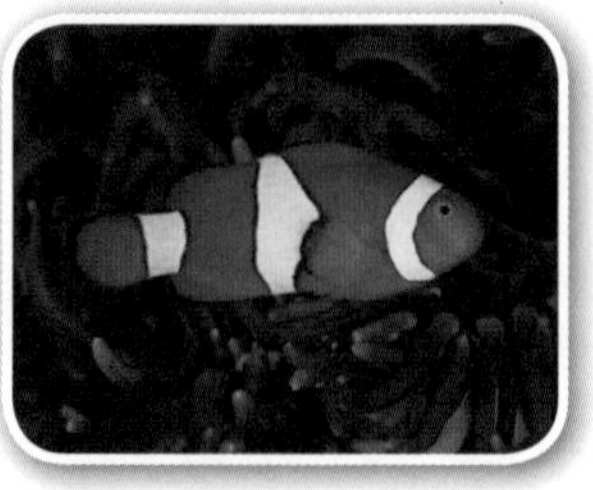

yú
鱼

yǎng
养

wèi
喂

qīng lǐ
清理

dòng wù yuán
动物园

gōng yuán
公园

huā yuán
花园
(garden)

niǎo yuán
鸟园
(bird park; aviary)

Search It on the Net

1 The Chinese Zodiac ("十二生肖" (shēng xiào)) is a cycle of twelve animal signs that the Chinese uses to calculate time by years. Use the Internet to find out what the twelve Zodiac animals are, and what your sign is.

2 Which other countries also make use of animal signs to keep tab on years? Find out the similarities and differences between these and the Chinese Zodiac.

New Words

dòng wù 动物 animal	gǒu 狗 dog	māo 猫 cat	
niǎo 鸟 bird	yú 鱼 fish	yǎng 养 raise	wèi 喂 feed
qīng lǐ 清理 clean	dòng wù yuán 动物园 zoo	gōng yuán 公园 park	

Let's CHANT

Go 400

dòng wù yuán
我有小小动物园，

māo gǒu xiǎo niǎo yú
猫狗小鸟还有鱼，

wèi tā men
每天喂它们吃饭，

qīng lǐ dà xiǎo biàn
还要清理大小便。

TIP! In the past, animals were kept in Chinese households mainly because of their usefulness. For example, dogs served as watchdogs and buffaloes helped to till the fields. Nowadays, however, it is common for many Chinese to keep animals and take care of them as pets, perhaps due to Western influence.

New Words

tā men
它们 they (referring to animals and objects)

dà xiǎo biàn
大小便 feces and urine

Let's Learn GRAMMAR

我	带	狗 (gǒu)	去	散步。

我们带花去看老师。

奶奶生病了，爸爸带奶奶去看病。

明天要比赛了，他们带球去体育馆练习。

TIP In this sentence pattern, the structure is "subject + 带 (take) + noun (someone or something) + 去 + verb (do something)". "去" is typically placed before the verb which indicates the action. To indicate the place where the action takes place, the location should be placed between "去" and the verb.

是谁	带狗 (gǒu) 去散步	的？

是谁喂(wèi)鱼(yú)的？

是谁教你唱歌的？

是谁帮你洗衣服的？

是谁带你来体育馆的？

TIP Adding "是" before "谁" will convey a question in a more forceful tone.

Expansion of Sentences

yǎng yú
哥哥在家里养鱼。

yǎng yú
哥哥在家里养了很多鱼。

yǎng yú
哥哥在家里养了很多不同的鱼。

huā yuán
奶奶在花园里种花。

huā yuán
奶奶在花园里种了很多花。

huā yuán
奶奶在花园里种了很多美丽的花。

他在餐厅里吃三明治。

他在餐厅里吃了四个三明治。

他在餐厅里吃了四个好吃的三明治。

Want More Practice?

Model after the sample sentences to expand the following:

(1) 我在教室里看书。
(2) 外公送我生日礼物。

Go400

WANT TO LEARN MORE?

Check out the Text > Sentence Pattern section in the Go400 CD.

Let's TALK

Find a partner and practice the following dialogues.

Task 1

xiǎo gǒu
A: 你喜欢小狗吗？

xiǎo gǒu　kě ài
B: 喜欢，因为小狗很可爱。

xiǎo gǒu
A: 我喜欢带小狗去散步。我在前面跑，

xiǎo gǒu　yǎng xiǎo gǒu
小狗在后面跑，很好玩。可是养小狗要

qīng lǐ tā dà xiǎo biàn
清理它的大小便，我不喜欢。

yǎng tā　tā
B: 养它就要照顾它。

Task 2

yǎng　zhī māo
A: 大关说你家养了三只猫。

yǎng māo
B: 没错！除了养猫，

yǎng　tiáo yú
我家还养了十条鱼。

māo　yú
A: 卡通里的猫都喜欢吃鱼，

māo　yú
你家的猫也喜欢吃鱼吗？

B: ______________________________。

New Words

kě ài
可爱 adorable, cute

zhī
只 (a measure word for animals or birds)

tiáo
条 (a measure word for fish)

Task 3

zhī xiǎo gǒu

A: 上个星期我姐姐带了一只小狗回家。

xiǎo gǒu

小狗是朋友送她的生日礼物。

xiǎo gǒu

B: 是谁照顾小狗的？

tā qīng lǐ dà xiǎo biàn

A: 我每天放学回家就帮它清理大小便。

wèi xiǎo gǒu

B: 是谁喂小狗的？

wèi tā xiǎo gǒu

A: 我妈妈每天喂它。小狗吃得很少，

很快就吃饱了。

B: 你姐姐做什么？

xiǎo gǒu gōng yuán

A: 姐姐每天带小狗去公园散步。

Task 4

yǎng dòng wù

A: 你喜欢养小动物吗？

B: ______________________________。

A: 为什么？

B: ______________________________。

The following dialogues are adapted from the Text > Dialogue section in your Go 400. Listen to the CD before reading the transcript on this page.

Task 5

yǎng dòng wù
A: 你有没有养小动物？

yǎng zhī gǒu
B: 有，我养了一只狗。

gǒu
A: 你家的狗，是谁照顾的？

wèi tā
B: 是我照顾的，我每天要喂它，

tā dà xiǎo biàn
还要带它出去大小便。

yǎng gǒu
A: 养狗容易吗？

ài xīn
B: 有爱心 (a kind heart) 就容易。

Task 6

yǎng tiáo yú
A: 你养了几条鱼？

yǎng tiáo yú
B: 我养了六条鱼。

Want More Practice?

Develop the dialogue in Task 6 in the same manner as the dialogue in Task 5. Ask B:

- Who takes care of his pet fish?
- How does the person take care of the pet fish?
- Is keeping a pet fish an easy task?

Let's Learn CHARACTER

Origin of Chinese Characters

Some Chinese characters originated directly from pictorial illustrations of objects and hence are known as "象形字" (xiàng xíng zì) (pictographic characters).

The tortoise in China is a symbol for longevity and auspicious tidings. In ancient China, tortoises were also used when people sought predictions from divine providence. The predictions received were then inscribed on the flat underside of tortoise shells. These writings formed China's earliest writings and are known as "甲骨文" (jiǎ gǔ wén) (writings on tortoise shells or bones of other animals).

Match and Write

The following pictographic characters have evolved from early illustrations of animals. Can you figure out what animal each character represent? Match the characters to the pictures and write the corresponding letters in the boxes provided. Write the English names of these animals in the brackets.

1 ☐ (   ) →  → 鳥 → 鸟 (niǎo)

2 ☐ (   ) →  → 魚 → 鱼 (yú)

3 ☐ (   ) →  → 象 (xiàng)

4 ☐ (   ) →  → 馬 → 马 (mǎ)

5 ☐ (   ) →  → 龜 → 龟 (guī)

A 

B 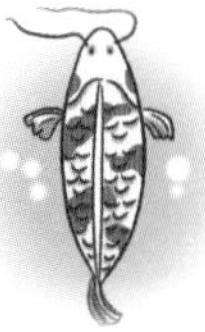

C 

D 

E 

F 

Let's READ

Text 1 Go400

Read the following text carefully.

我家是一个动物园(dòng wù yuán)，养(yǎng)了很多小动物(dòng wù)。哥哥的狗(gǒu)叫阳光，姐姐的猫(māo)叫圆球，我的小鸟(xiǎo niǎo)叫白雪，弟弟养(yǎng)了三条(tiáo)鱼(yú)，一条(tiáo)叫红红，一条(tiáo)叫白白，还有一条(tiáo)叫黑黑。

我们每天要喂(wèi)它(tā)们(men)，我们每天要清(qīng)理(lǐ)它(tā)们(men)的大(dà)小(xiǎo)便(biàn)，哥哥每天还要带阳光去散步。

我们都爱小动物(dòng wù)，我们都很用心地照顾小动物(dòng wù)。我们有爱(ài)心(xīn)，我们是它(tā)们(men)的爸爸妈妈。

Answer these questions in Chinese.

1 Why does the author say his house is like a zoo?

2 Why does the author say he and his siblings are the animals' parents?

3 In the table below, write down what animals the siblings own and their pets' names.

我 (the author)	哥哥	姐姐	弟弟
小鸟/白雪			

Go400

WANT TO LEARN MORE?

Check out the Text > Reading section in the Go400 CD.

Text 2

Read the following text carefully.

dòng wù yuán
上个星期日爸爸带我和弟弟去动物园。早上去
dòng wù yuán
动物园的人不多，票很快就买到了。

dòng wù yuán
动物园很大，有大树有草地。水里、树上、草
dòng wù yǎng dì fang
地上，不同的动物养在不同的地方*。

niǎo niǎo yuán yǎng niǎo
我喜欢鸟，鸟园里养了很多不同的鸟，有白色
yán sè niǎo
的，有红色的，还有蓝色的，什么颜色*的鸟都好看。
yú yú
弟弟喜欢鱼，爸爸就带他去看鱼。

下午我们在大树下休息。我一边吃着妈妈做的
dòng wù yuán dòng wù
三明治和果汁，一边想着动物园里的动物，今天真
是快乐的一天。

*地方 place *颜色 color

Answer these questions in Chinese.

1 With whom did the author go to the zoo? Which animal did he like most?

2 What are the colors of the birds in the aviary? Which one did the author find most attractive?

3 Number the following activities in the sequence they occurred in the passage.

看鱼	去动物园	吃三明治	大树下休息	买票	看鸟

Let's DO IT

Role Play

1 Form two teams. Team A assumes the role of a child and Team B assumes the role of the child's parents.

2 The child is requesting that his parents buy him a pet. However, his parents refuse to do so because they feel there is not enough space for the pet at their house. Besides, the child's enthusiasm for a pet might wane and the responsibility of taking care of the animal will then lie on the parents' shoulders.

3 An argument then ensues between the child and his parents.

(1) Decide what the animal is: ______________________________

(2) Team A (the child) is to list some reasons for having a pet.

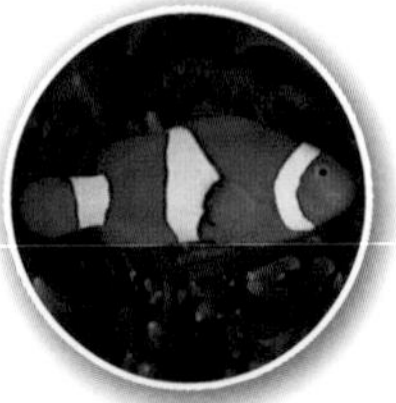

(3) Team B (the parents) is to list some problems that keeping a pet might cause.

4 After the discussion, each team is to send representatives up for a debate against the other team.

LEARNING LOG

I can...	Excellent	Good	Fair	Needs Improvement
1 name some common animals such as cat, dog, bird, and fish in Chinese.	☐	☐	☐	☐
2 describe what is required to look after small pets.	☐	☐	☐	☐
3 use the sentence structures "带……去……" and "是谁……的？" appropriately.	☐	☐	☐	☐
4 identify "鸟", "鱼", "象", "马", and "龟" as pictographic characters which evolved from illustrations.	☐	☐	☐	☐
5 write "狗", "猫", "鸟", "鱼", and "清".	☐	☐	☐	☐

LESSON

5

我的假期
My Vacation

My Goals

1 Be able to describe my travel plans
2 Be able to share my vacation experiences
3 Be able to express an inability to complete a task due to certain constraints
4 Be able to recognize that a Chinese character may have different meanings in different words and phrases
5 Become familiar with vocabulary associated with vacations

Get Started

Think About It

Are there any holidays or long weekends this semester? When is the next school holiday? What do you plan to do then?

一月

xīn nián jià qī
新年假期
(New Year holidays)

三月

chūn jià / lù yíng
春假/露营
(camp)

六月、七月、八月

shǔ jià / dǎ gōng
暑假/打工

十二月

hán jià / lǚ xíng
寒假/旅行

十二月

shèng dàn jià qī
圣诞假期/
(Christmas holidays)
qīn yǒu
看亲友

一月~十二月

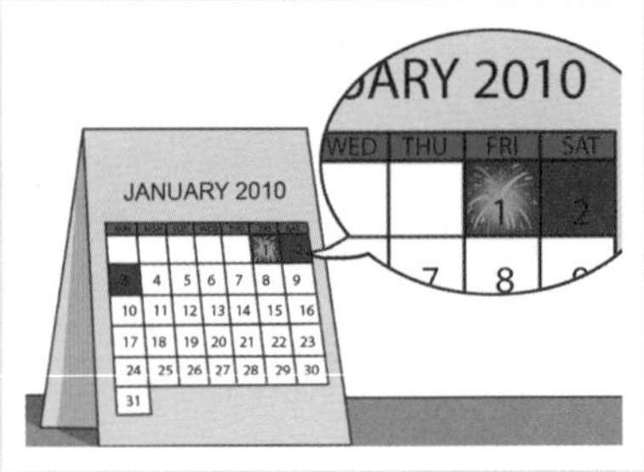

zhōu mò、zhōu mò
周末、长周末/
(long weekend)
运动

New Words

jià qī 假期 vacation	chūn jià 春假 spring break	shǔ jià 暑假 summer vacation	dǎ gōng 打工 have a part-time job
hán jià 寒假 winter vacation	lǚ xíng 旅行 travel	qīn yǒu 亲友 friends and relatives	zhōu mò 周末 weekend

Let's CHANT

Go 400

TIP

"打工" holds different meanings in different areas. In some places, it means to hold a temporary job during one's spare time. In other places, it means to be employed on a full-time basis. Be sure to check what it means if someone uses the term!

zhōu mò
长周末，可休息，

fàng chūn jià　qīn yǒu
放春假，看亲友。

shǔ jià　dǎ gōng
长长暑假可打工，

jià qī　lǚ xíng
长长假期去旅行。

New Words

fàng jià
放(假) take day(s) off

Let's Learn GRAMMAR

bié　bié rén　bié de
别 / 别人 / 别的

bié
电视好看，可是别看太久。

bié
别忘了下个星期二是我的生日。

dǎ gōng　lèi　bié　dǎ gōng
哥哥说在餐厅打工太累了，他希望我别去那里打工。

bié rén
这是别人的狗，不是我的狗。

bié rén
这是别人的书，我们不能拿。

bié rén zhōu mò　dǎ gōng　dǎ gōng
别人周末都在打工，我也想打工。

bié de
别的学校都有体育馆，可是我的学校没有。

bié de
这双鞋太贵了，你买别的好不好？

New Words

bié
别 don't

lèi
累 tired

bié rén
别人 other people

bié de
别的 other

TIP

"别 + verb" means "do not". "别 + measure word + noun" or "别的" means "(something) else". In deciphering which meaning "别" holds in a sentence, one should read the phrases before and after it.

zhǐ yǒu
只有

zhǐ yǒu
只有我知道。

zhǐ yǒu
只有他会开车。

"只有" here means "only".

TIP

"只有" has two functions.
1. As an adverb, "只有" means "exclusively" or "only".
2. In the phrase "只 + 有", "只" modifies the verb "有" and expresses a limit of what is available.

zhǐ yǒu jià
我只有两天假。

zhǐ yǒu
我只有十块钱。

Here, "只有" indicates a limit of what is available.

我	zhǐ yǒu 只有	jià 两天假，	不够	lǚ xíng 去旅行	的。

zhǐ yǒu
教室只有一台电脑，不够大家用的。

zhǐ yǒu
表弟只有五块钱，不够买书的。

zhǐ yǒu
大关只有八块钱，不够去餐厅吃饭的。

New Words

zhǐ yǒu
只有 only

jià
假 vacation; break; leave

TIP

The structure "只有……，不够……的" indicates an inability to complete a task due to certain constraints. "只有" here introduces the limited conditions or objects which cause the incompleteness of a task.

Go400

WANT TO LEARN MORE?

Check out the Text > Sentence Pattern section in the Go400 CD.

Let's TALK

Find a partner and practice the following dialogues.

Task 1

xīn nián jià qī
A: 每年新年假期时，我都会去看奶奶。

guó jiā　xīn nián
B: 每个国家(country)的新年都是一月一日吗？

guó jiā　xīn nián
A: 不是。有的国家有自己的新年，

rì qī
每年的日期(date)都不一样。

TIP

In China, the Lunar New Year is celebrated with a long holiday, usually around January or February. Since schools typically break for the winter vacation around the same time, students get to enjoy a long vacation then.

Task 2

shǔ jià　dǎ gōng
A: 暑假我要去打工，你要做什么？

rì běn　lǚ xíng　zhōng guó　qīn yǒu
B: 我要去日本(Japan)旅行，还要去中国看亲友。

lǚ xíng
你要不要和我一起去旅行？

shǔ jià　zhǐ yǒu
A: 这个暑假，我只有两天能休息，

lǚ xíng
不够去旅行的。

Task 3

shǔ jià dǎ gōng
A：妈，暑假我想去打工。

dǎ gōng
B：你想去哪里打工？

bié rén dǎ gōng
A：别人都去学校打工，我也想去。

dǎ gōng
B：在学校打工要做什么？

A：我要打字，还要带新同学认识学校。

bié lèi
B：你可以去，可是别太累了。

A：我知道，谢谢妈！

Task 4

zhōu mò
A：你这个周末要做什么？

B：______________________。

A：你自己一个人去吗？

B：______________________。

The following dialogues can be found in the Text > Dialogue section in your Go400. Listen to the CD before reading the transcript on this page.

Task 5

fàng shǔ jià
A: 你什么时候开始放暑假？

fàng shǔ jià
B: 我们从六月二十一号开始放暑假。

shǔ jià
A: 暑假你要做什么？

shǔ jià dǎ gōng
B: 今年暑假我想去餐厅打工。

dǎ gōng
A: 去餐厅打工，一个小时多少钱？

B: 那是我叔叔的餐厅，赚多少钱不重要，我可以学做事。

Task 6

zhōu mò
A: 这个周末你要不要来我家玩？

xíng zhōu mò xíng
B: 不行，我下个星期要交很多作业，下个周末行吗？

Want More Practice?

Create two new dialogues by changing B's responses in Tasks 5 and 6.

New Words

xíng
行 can

Let's Learn PHRASE

Characters with Multiple Meanings

In Chinese morphology, characters are meaningfully combined to create words and phrases. The same character may appear in a number of words and phrases, but its meaning may differ. Look at the common character in the words and phrases below. Try to figure out its meaning in each of them and write it down in the brackets provided.

TIP

"打" has a myriad of meanings. It can mean:

- an action involving a tapping motion, like "打字" (typing);
- combat, like "打架" (fight);
- sending out something, like "打电话" (calling somebody on the telephone);
- play, like "打球" (play ball);
- work, like "打工" (work).

How many uses of "打" do you know?

打

打字 → (typing)

打架 → (fighting)

打电话 → (make a phone-call)

打球 → (play ball)

dǎ gōng
打工 → (working)

开

开心 → (happy)

开车 → (drive a car)

打开 → (open)

Characters with Multiple Pronunciations

In some cases, the same character in different words and phrases may be pronounced differently. When a character has a different pronunciation, it usually signals a difference in the meaning as well. Recall the examples of "便宜" and "方便", which we have learned before. Write down the *pinyin* of the words and phrases below and their English translation.

长

校长 → (xiào zhǎng) → (principal)

长大 → (zhǎng da) → (growing up)

长高 → (zhǎng gao) → (grow taller)

长假期 → (chang zāi chí) → (long holiday)

长桌子 → (chang zhī zí) → ( )

Let's READ

Text 1 Go400

Read the following text carefully.

我们上学很辛苦，可是，我们有周末(zhōu mò)，有春假(chūn jià)，有暑假(shǔ jià)，还有很多假期(jià qī)可以休息。

爸爸上班很辛苦，可是，爸爸有周末(zhōu mò)，爸爸有年假(nián jià)*，还有很多假期(jià qī)可以休息。

只有(zhǐ yǒu)妈妈最辛苦，不放假(fàng jià)，不休息；每天从早忙到晚，春夏秋冬都在忙。别(bié)忘了，妈妈也要假期(jià qī)，妈妈也要休息。

* 年假 annual vacation

Answer these questions in Chinese.

1 What vacations does the author's father have? What can he do on these vacations?

2 Why does the author's mother not have any vacation? What can he do to allow his mother to take a break?

3 According to the passage, what vacations do students and working adults have? Check the appropriate boxes in the table below.

	春假	暑假	年假	周末
上学的人	✓	✓		✓
上班的人			✓	✓

4 Check the box next to the most appropriate title for the passage.

☐ 给妈妈一个假期 ☐ 上学真辛苦！ ☐ 有假期可以休息

Text 2

Read the following text carefully.

fàng jià lǚ xíng
放假了，真开心，爸爸要带我们去旅行。

lǚ xíng qián qǐng rén
旅行前*，我们很忙：妈妈要请人*照顾猫狗，

qǐng rén
爸爸要请人照顾花草，我们也得做完功课。

lǚ xíng lù
旅行的时候，我们也很忙：要找路*、要找饭

lǚ xíng
馆、找厕所。妈妈说旅行和在家不一样，做什么都

要小心。

lǚ xíng lèi
旅行完，回到家，大家都很累，大家都说回到

lǚ xíng lèi lǚ xíng
家真好。旅行很累，可是很快乐。我喜欢去旅行，

jiā rén lǚ xíng
更喜欢和家人*一起去旅行。

*前 before *请人 ask someone

*路 road *家人 family member

Answer these questions in Chinese.

1 What did everybody have to do before the trip?

2 What did everybody have to do during the trip?

3 Why did everybody proclaim "回家真好" at the end of the trip?

Go400

WANT TO LEARN MORE?

Check out the Text > Reading section in the Go400 CD.

Let's DO IT

1 What do you plan to do over the next long vacation? Use the following dialogue to interview your classmates to find out their plans.

大关：小明，寒假(hán jià)你想做什么？

小明：我想去图书馆打工(dǎ gōng)。

大关：在图书馆打工(dǎ gōng)要做什么？

小明：我会打字，我可以帮图书馆把书名打在电脑里。

You may also use these questions in your interview.

- 去________打工，一个小时多少钱？
- 你要学什么？一个星期要上几次课？
- 你要去哪里旅行？你要和谁去？

2 Gather the responses of the entire class. What do most of your classmates plan on doing over the long vacation?

LEARNING LOG

I can...	Excellent	Good	Fair	Needs Improvement
1 name some common vacations such as the winter vacation and the summer vacation.	☐	☐	☐	☐
2 describe my plans for my vacation and share my vacation experiences.	☐	☐	☐	☐
3 use the sentence structure "只有……，不够……的" to explain the reason for one's inability to complete a task.	☐	☐	☐	☐
4 recognize that "打", "开", and "长" have different meanings in different words and phrases.	☐	☐	☐	☐
5 write "放", "假", "工", "别", and "累".	☐	☐	☐	☐

LESSON

6

我家房间
Rooms in My Home

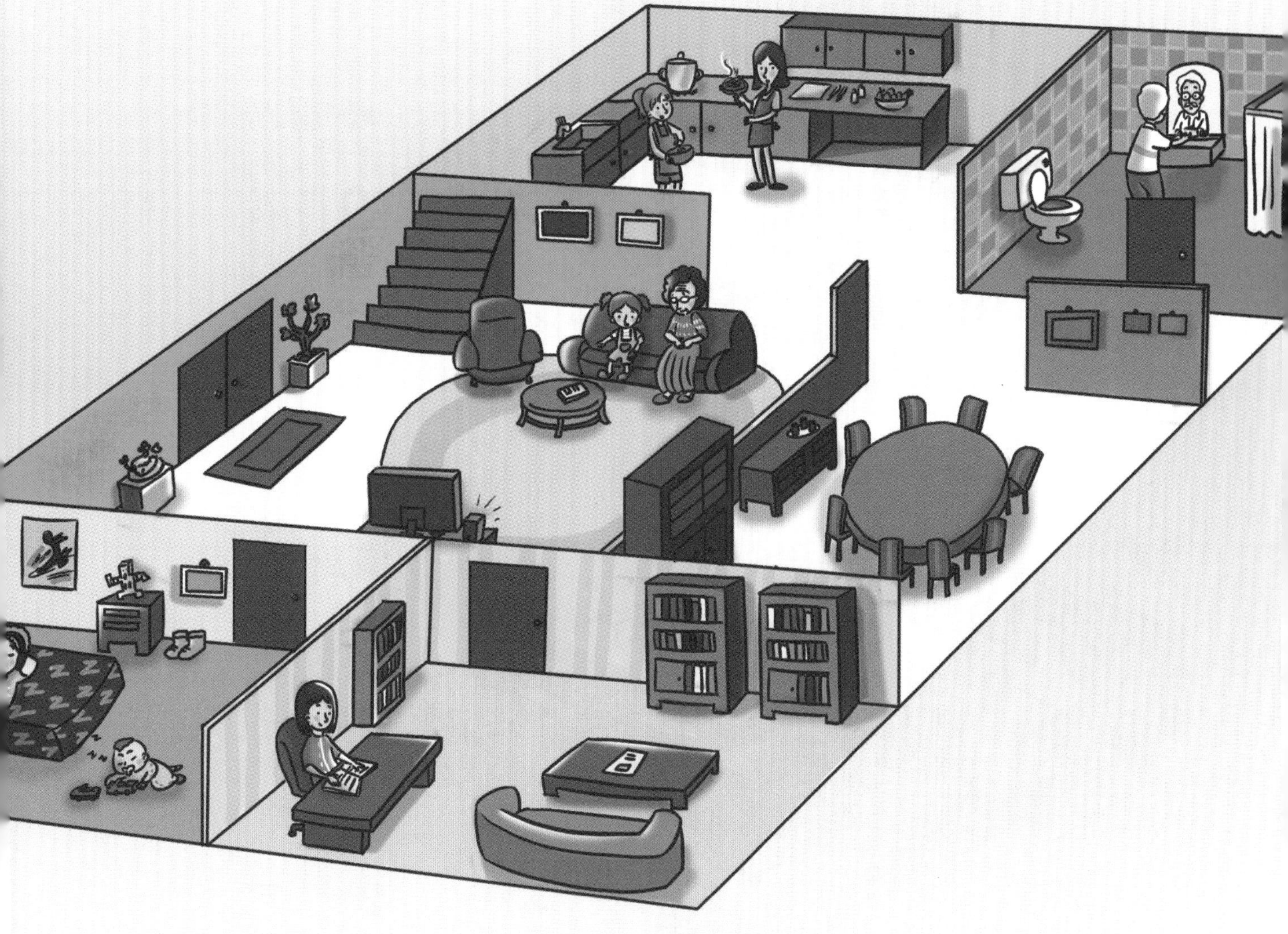

My Goals

1 Be able to name the different rooms in my house and their functions
2 Be able to indicate the completion of an action
3 Be able to recognize that an independent character may have a different meaning when it becomes part of a word or phrase
4 Become familiar with vocabulary associated with the rooms of a house and their uses

Get Started

fáng jiān
我家的房间。

Show and Tell

1 Draw a floor plan of your house. How many rooms are there in your house? How many people live in your house? Share the information with your classmates.

2 Name three rooms in your house that you spend the most time in, and tell your classmates what you enjoy doing most in these rooms.

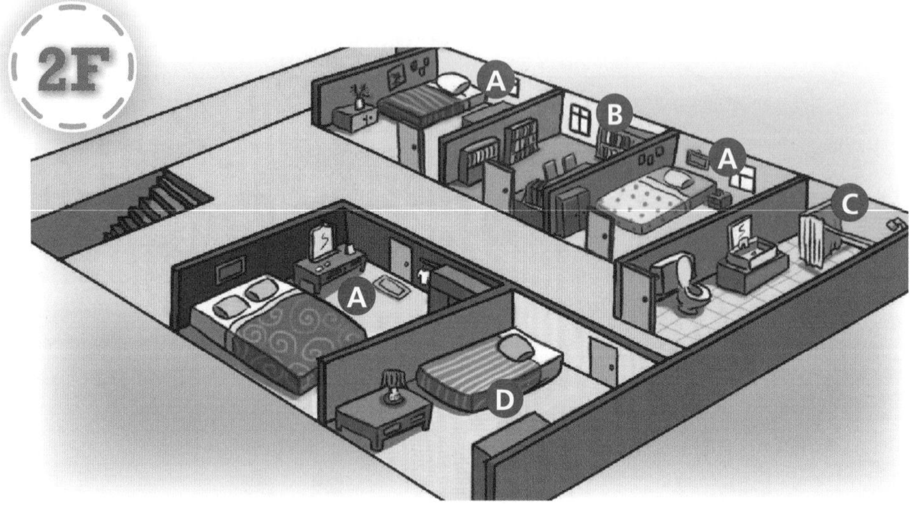

shuì fáng
A 睡房

shū fáng
B 书房

yù shì
C 浴室

kè fáng
D 客房

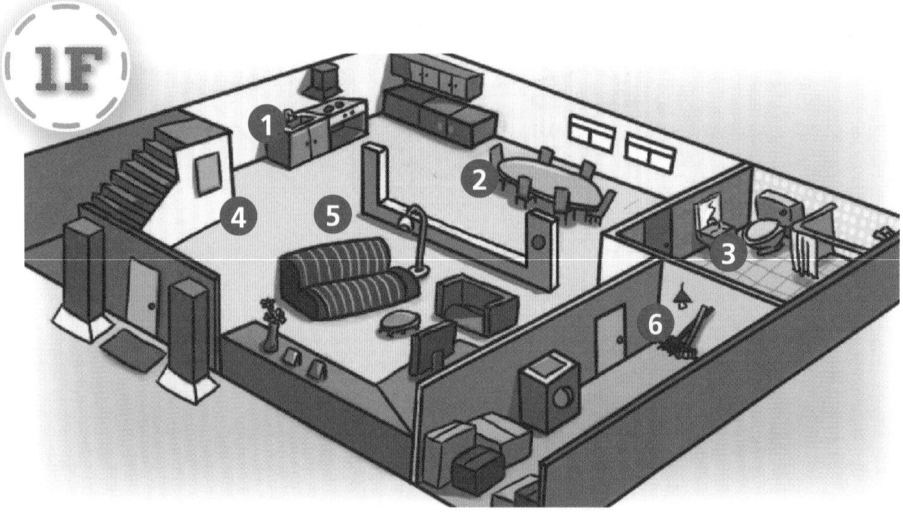

chú fáng
1 厨房

fàn tīng
2 饭厅

3 厕所

lóu tī
4 楼梯 (stairs)

kè tīng
5 客厅

chú cáng shì
6 储藏室 (storeroom)

New Words

fáng jiān 房间 room	kè tīng 客厅 living room	fàn tīng 饭厅 dining room	chú fáng 厨房 kitchen
shuì fáng 睡房 bedroom	shū fáng 书房 study	kè fáng 客房 guest room	yù shì 浴室 bathroom

Let's CHANT

Go 400

kè rén　　　　kè tīng
客人来了客厅坐，

chú fáng　　　fàn tīng
厨房做饭饭厅吃，

shū fáng　　　　shuì fáng
书房旁边是睡房，

xǐ zǎo shàng chuáng shuì jiào
洗澡上床去睡觉。

Find It

"睡房", also known as "卧室" (wò shì), means the bedroom. In the picture on page 61, who can you see in the "睡房"?

TIP

Many Chinese who believe in *fengshui* believe that the direction a house faces, the layout of the house, and even the positions of the ornaments and furniture in the house influence the owner's aura and luck. This may sound incredulous, but some of these beliefs may have sound, scientific logic. For example, the belief against placing a mirror in front of one's bed is rather logical – it may prevent the person from being scared by his own reflection when he wakes up!

New Words

kè rén 客人 guest	zuò 坐 sit	xǐ zǎo 洗澡 take a bath	shàng chuáng 上床 go to bed	shuì jiào 睡觉 sleep

Let's Learn GRAMMAR

	xǐ		zǎo
弟弟	洗	过	澡了。

dōng xi
我吃过东西了。

妹妹去过动物园了。

A: 你看过我的书？
B: 我看过你的书了。

A: 你有没有看过这个节目？
B: 我没看过这个节目。

A: 你玩过这个电脑游戏吗？
B: 我没玩过这个电脑游戏。

TIP "Verb + 过" indicates the completion of an action. The action could be in the past or the future.
For example:
➤ 弟弟洗过澡了。(past)
➤ 明天我吃过饭就去你家。(future)
To give a negative reply to a question with the structure "verb + 过", one can simply use "没(有)".
➤ 我没(有)玩过电脑游戏。

New Words

dōng xi
东西 thing

Go400 **WANT TO LEARN MORE?**
Check out the Text > Sentence Pattern section in the Go400 CD.

jīng guò
经过

location

jīng guò
从这里到办公室，你会经过我的教室。

jīng guò
从我家到运动场，你会经过学校。

time

jīng guò
经过很多年，他长大了。

jīng guò
经过两年，我会写很多中文字了。

New Words

jīng guò
经过 pass by

TIP
The phrase "经过" is similar to the sentence structure "从……到……" in that they express either location or time. One needs the context of the entire sentence to determine which meaning the phrases "经过" expresses.

Repetition of Measure Word
一 + Measure Word + 一 + Measure Word

弟弟学走路，怎么走？

一步一步走。

这本书有很多课，怎么学？

一课一课学。

妹妹问我很多问题，怎么回答？

一题一题回答。

TIP
Measure words are repeated to show that an action is rather unexceptional and routine. When it is placed before a verb, it can exemplify the step-by-step manner in which the action is undertaken.

Let's TALK

Find a partner and practice the following dialogues.

Task 1

dōng xī
A: 今天上中文课，我学了“东”、“西”两个字。

dōng xi
B: 我知道，除了人和动物，什么都是“东西”。

dōng xī yì si yì si
A: “东”、“西”除了这个意思(meaning)，还有别的意思。

B: 你可以用这两个字说一个句子吗？

dōng biān xī biān
A: 可以。“早上太阳在东边，下午太阳在西边。”

Task 2

fáng zi shū fáng
A: 我家房子(house)很小，没有书房。

B: 你在哪里写作业？

kè tīng
A: 我在客厅写作业。

kè fáng
B: 你家有客房吗？

kè rén shuì kè tīng
A: 没有，客人来了就得睡在客厅。

kè tīng
B: 你家客厅真有用。

New Words

dōng biān
东边 east

xī biān
西边 west

Task 3

A: 我昨天很晚睡觉（shuì jiào），只睡（shuì）了六个小时。

B: 为什么？

A: 我看电影看得太晚了。

B: 我昨晚洗（xǐ）完澡上床（zǎo shàng chuáng），也十一点了。

A: 为什么你也很晚睡（shuì），你昨晚也在看电影吗？

B: 我没看电影。昨晚我在写作业，一题一题用心写，写完就十点半了。

Task 4

A: 你每天上学，会经过（jīng guò）公园吗？

B: ____________________。

A: 你看过公园里的花了吗？

B: ____________________。

Task 5

Can you identify the pairs of dialogue from the eight utterances below? Organize them into four dialogues and fill in the following table. When this is done, you may listen to the Text > Dialogue section in your Go400 for the correct answers.

1	A:	2	A:	3	A:	4	A:
	B:		B:		B:		B:

qǐng jìn　qǐng zuò

❶ 请进！请坐！请问你要喝什么？

❷ 吃过了，你还没有吃吗？

❸ 鞋子是七号半，衣服是大号。

❹ 谢谢！请给我一杯果汁。

jiān

❺ 我家是三百二十一号，就是左边那一间，前面有大树。

❻ 你穿几号的鞋子？几号的衣服？

❼ 你家是几号？

❽ 吃过饭了吗？

New Words

qǐng jìn
请进 please come in

jiān
间 (a measure word for room, house, etc.)

Let's Learn PHRASE

The meaning of a single character frequently changes when it becomes part of a word or phrase. This lesson illustrates the case of "东 (dōng)" and "西 (xī)".

东 (dōng) 西 (xī)

Individually, "东 (dōng)" and "西 (xī)" are prepositions of location which means "east" and "west".

东西 (dōng xi)

Together, "东西 (dōng xi)" as a word means "thing".

图书馆在学校的东边 (dōng biān)，体育馆在学校的西边 (xī biān)。

我家的西边 (xī biān) 是学校，东边 (dōng biān) 是医院。

他的睡房 (shuì fáng) 里东西 (dōng xi) 很多。

妈妈去买东西 (dōng xi) 了，她不在家。

TIP Be careful not to use the term "东西" to refer to a person, such as "你是什么东西？" and "你不是东西。". Coupled with an inappropriate tone, it may sound like a reprimand and may lead to misunderstandings!

Expressing Direction and Location

In Chinese, "东南西北 (dōng nán xī běi)" are used for indicating the four cardinal directions — east, south, west, and north. For the intermediate directions, the Chinese expressions are different from the English expressions. Can you tell the difference?

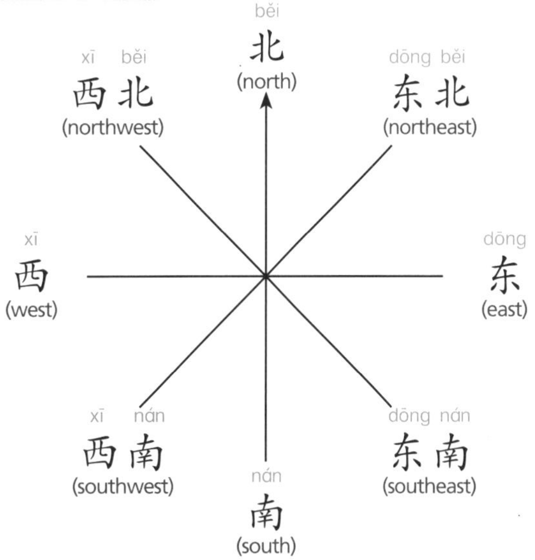

Let's READ

Text 1

Read the following text carefully.

家，有客厅(kè tīng)，客人(kè rén)来了，我们和客人(kè rén)在客厅坐(kè tīng zuò)下来，说说话，看看电视。

家，有饭厅(fàn tīng)，桌子上有妈妈的爱心，大家坐(zuò)在一起，吃着说着，真开心。

家，有睡房(shuì fáng)，我有我的小天地(tiān dì)*，我喜欢在里面玩电脑、打电话、睡觉，也可以什么都不做。

家，是我们休息的地方(dì fang)*，也是我们最爱的地方(dì fang)。

*天地 world　　*地方 place

Answer these questions in Chinese.

1 What do you think "妈妈的爱心" refers to? How do you know?

2 Fill in the blanks with the areas of the house mentioned by the author.

3 Which area in his house does the author like most? Which area in your house do you like most?

Go400

WANT TO LEARN MORE?

Check out the Text > Reading section in the Go400 CD.

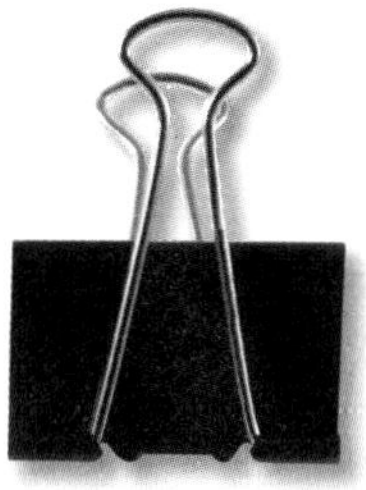

Text 2

Read the following text carefully.

shuì fáng　fáng jiān

我的睡房是我家最大的房间。那里有很多书、

chuáng

一张大桌子，还有一张大床*。

chuáng　shuì

我的大床可以睡两个人，有时同学来我家，我

tǎng　chuáng　liáo tiān

们就躺*在大床上聊天*。

chuáng　dōng xi

我的床下有很多好玩的东西：有球赛的票，有

zhào piàn

我跳舞的照片*，还有我的生日礼物。

rì jì běn　chuáng　rì jì

我的日记本*也在床下。我不希望别人知道日记

běn　chuáng xià　rì jì běn

本在床下。我最不希望爸妈知道日记本在那里。

*床 bed　*躺 lie down　*聊天 chat　*照片 photo　*日记本 diary

Answer these questions in Chinese.

1 According to the text, which of the following descriptions is accurate?

☐ 我的床是家里最大的。　☐ 我有很多东西在床下。

☐ 我最喜欢爸妈看我的日记本。

2 Where in his room does the author like to chat with his friends?

3 Which sequence accurately depicts the order in which the items were mentioned in the text?

☐ 睡房 → 床 → 床下 → 日记本

☐ 房间 → 照片 → 睡房 → 日记本

☐ 睡房 → 床下 → 床上 → 日记本

This sequence introduces items from _____ to _____. (大/小)

Let's DO IT

1 In the box below, draw the floor plan of your house as demonstrated in the example below. Write three descriptive sentences about your house in the spaces provided.

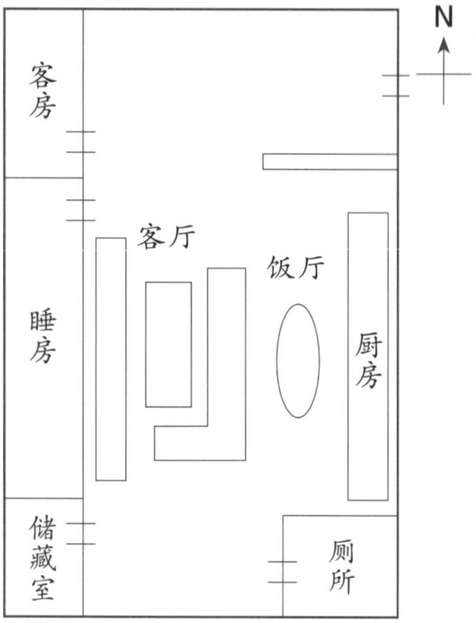

①

②

③

2 Form groups of three. Compare your floor plans to identify three similarities and three differences, and present them to the class.

LEARNING LOG

I can...	Excellent	Good	Fair	Needs Improvement
1 describe the rooms in my house.	☐	☐	☐	☐
2 state the purpose of different rooms in my house.	☐	☐	☐	☐
3 use "verb + 过" to indicate the completion of an action.	☐	☐	☐	☐
4 explain the difference between "东西" as a word, and "东" and "西" as individual characters.	☐	☐	☐	☐
5 write "房", "间", "东", "西", and "坐".	☐	☐	☐	☐

LESSON

7

我用筷子
Using Chopsticks

My Goals

1 Know more about the differences between Chinese and Western dining
2 Be able to express an action imposed on an object and the result of the action on the object
3 Be able to describe adjectives in greater detail with the adverb "好"
4 Be able to use the appropriate measure word for various tableware items
5 Become familiar with the names of various tableware items used in Chinese and Western dining

Get Started

kuài zi
筷子

tāng chí tāng sháo
汤匙/汤勺

Play It

Divide into two teams for this game. Each team is to prepare an identical set of vocabulary cards and scatter it on the respective tables. When the teacher recites a word, the representative from each team must locate the corresponding card on his table, pick it up with a pair of chopsticks, and transfer it to a plate. The faster team to do so wins.

dāo zi
刀子

chā zi
叉子

wǎn
碗

pán zi
盘子

guō
锅
(pot)

饭

菜

tāng
汤

New Words

kuài zi 筷子 chopsticks	tāng chí tāng sháo 汤匙/汤勺 spoon	dāo zi 刀子 knife

chā zi 叉子 fork	wǎn 碗 bowl	pán zi 盘子 plate	tāng 汤 soup

Let's CHANT

Go 400

Holding Chopsticks

1 Pick up one chopstick. Position it such that one end rests on the part between your thumb and your index finger, and the other end rests on your ring finger.

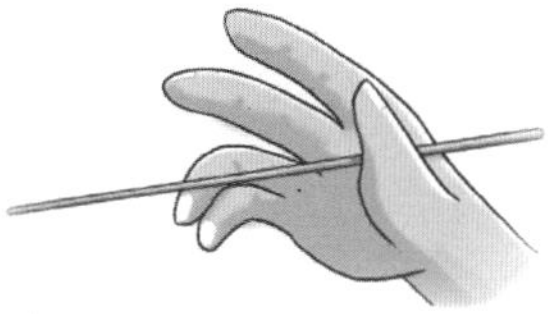

2 Place the other chopstick gently between your index and middle fingertips. Move your thumb toward your index finger and grip the chopstick firmly.

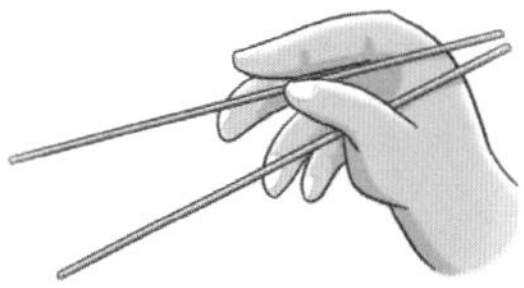

3 The chopsticks should be neatly aligned, and the ends for picking food up just touching each other. Hold the first chopstick stationary while moving the second one with your thumb, index, and middle fingers. With practice, you will be rather adept at picking things up with a pair of chopsticks.

zhōng cān kuài zi
吃中餐，用筷子，

xī cān dāo chā
吃西餐，用刀叉，

wǎn pán tāng chí
碗盘汤匙都有用，

kǒu kǒu màn màn
一口一口慢慢吃。

TIP

Traditionally, the Chinese had a penchant for eating food warm and cooking vegetables and meat with water to create dishes with broth. It was impractical to consume such dishes with bare hands or a knife. Hence, the Chinese made, out of bamboo or tree bark, what we now consider an integral piece of cutlery in Chinese dining — chopsticks.

In Chinese dining where many people are seated around the table, the etiquette of dining is as important as the food. It is therefore important to know the etiquette of using chopsticks. For example, the chopsticks should not be used to point at somebody, or to stir one's food. One should neither stick his/her chopsticks into his/her food nor separate them on either side of the bowl, like he/she would do with a fork and knife.

New Words

zhōng cān 中餐 Chinese food	xī cān 西餐 Western food	kǒu 口 mouthful	màn 慢 slow

Let's Learn GRAMMAR

bǎ
把

tāng　　　　　　　　bǎ tāng
我喝完汤了。→ 我把汤喝完了。

　　　　　　　　　　　bǎ
他做完功课了。→ 他把功课做完了。

　　　wǎn　　　　　　　bǎ wǎn
哥哥洗好碗了。→ 哥哥把碗洗好了。

　　bǎ　　fàng
奶奶把礼物放在我的睡房里。

bǎ kuài zi fàng
我把筷子放在厨房里。

TIP

A sentence consisting of "把" is typically made up of five segments:
subject + 把 + object + verb + complement

我	把	汤	喝	完了。
他	把	鞋子	穿	好了。

This construction indicates the object, the action imposed on it, and the result of the action on the object.

　　　　bǎ wǎn
吃完饭要把碗洗好。

　　qián　　　　bǎ
睡觉前 (before) 要把作业写完。

New Words

bǎ
把 (used before an object and followed by a verb)

fàng
放 put

zhōng cān xī cān 中餐、西餐	都可以，	我	都	喜欢。

打桌球、打棒球都可以，我们都会。

养猫、养狗都可以，外婆都喜欢。

去公园、去运动场都可以，我都知道怎么去。

TIP In this structure, "都" encompasses all the subjects mentioned. It is usually used in responding questions, suggesting that all the options stated are acceptable.

好

那本书好贵。

这只小狗好可爱。

kuài zi
筷子好难拿，我拿得不好。

今天的作业好多，我写了好久。

昨天我生日，大家送了好多礼物给我。

TIP "好" can be used as an adjective or an adverb. As an adverb, it is commonly placed before another adjective to express a greater degree.

Go400 WANT TO LEARN MORE?

Check out the Text > Sentence Pattern section in the Go400 CD.

Let's TALK

Find partner(s) and practice the following dialogues.

Task 1

zhōng cān xī cān

A: 你要吃中餐还是西餐？

zhōng cān xī cān

B: 中餐、西餐都可以，我都喜欢。

zhōng cān

A: 前面那家餐厅的中餐很好吃，可是得用

kuài zi

筷子吃。

kuài zi dāo chā

B: 筷子、刀叉都可以，我都会用。

zhōng cān

A: 太好了！我们去那家餐厅吃中餐。

Task 2

A: 你好，请问你们几个人？

B: ________________。

A: 请你们等一等，我请

fú wù yuán

服务员 (waiter) 带你们进去。

C: 这边请。

Task 3

A: 请问你们要吃什么？

wǎn
B: 我要吃面，请给我一碗面。

wǎn pán
C: 我要吃饭。我要一碗饭，还要一盘菜和一
wǎn tāng
碗汤。

wǎn wǎn
D: 我也要吃面。我们一共要两碗面、一碗饭、
pán wǎn tāng
一盘菜和一碗汤。

Task 4

kuài zi
A: 你拿筷子拿得真好。

kuài zi
B: 因为我每天都用筷子吃饭。

zhōng cān kuài zi
A: 我喜欢吃中餐，可是我拿筷子拿得不好。
你可以教我吗？

kuài zi
B: 可以。拿筷子不难，你用心地练习就会了。

Task 5

A: 我把(bǎ)饭吃完了，也把(bǎ)菜吃完了。

B: 我也把(bǎ)面吃完了。

C: 我们还有汤(tāng)，大家一起来喝汤(tāng)！

> **TIP** Western dining is a rather individualized experience where each person orders and consumes his/her own dish. Chinese dining is more about sharing, where everybody partakes of the same dishes on the table.

The following dialogues can be found in the Text > Dialogue section in your Go400. Listen to the CD before reading the transcript on this page.

Task 6

A: 你想吃中餐(zhōng cān)还是西餐(xī cān)？

B: 都可以，请你选。

Task 7

A: 你要用筷子(kuài zi)还是刀叉(dāo chā)？

B: 我用筷子(kuài zi)用得不好，还是用刀叉(dāo chā)方便。

Task 8

A: 可不可以再给我一个碗(wǎn)？

B: 好的，没问题。

> "再" here means "again" or "more". It should not be confused with another use of "再", which means "then", as in "看完电影，再去图书馆。"

Let's Learn MEASURE WORD

Apart from their literal meaning of "bowl" and "plate", "碗 (wǎn)" and "盘 (pán)" are also measure words. Measure words are a unique feature of the Chinese language where different nouns have different measure words. Do you know the appropriate measure words for various tableware items and the dishes of a meal?

一张桌子。

wǎn tāng　　wǎn　　pán
一碗汤、两碗饭、三盘菜。

kuài zi　　bǎ dāo zi
四双筷子、一把刀子、

chā zi　　tāng chí
一个叉子、三个汤匙。

Practice It

Fill in the brackets with the correct measure word.

1. 一(　　)餐厅。
2. 一(　　)房间。
3. 一(　　)碗 (wǎn)、两(　　)盘子 (pán zi)。
4. 五(　　)饭、三(　　)菜。
5. 一(　　)小鱼。
6. 一(　　)狗。

New Words

bǎ
把 (a measure word for knife, etc.)

Let's READ

Text 1 Go400

Read the following sentences carefully.

pán pán màn màn

A 好多好多的菜，真好吃，一盘一盘慢慢吃。

B 好长好长的路，小心走，一步一步走得好。

C 好多好多本书，真好看，一本一本用心看。

màn màn

D 好多好多句子，慢慢说，一句一句说得好。

E 好多好多个字，用心写，一字一字写得好。

Answer these questions in Chinese.

1 Listen to the text on your CD. According to the CD, arrange the above sentences in the right order and write down the corresponding letters in the boxes below.

→ ☐ ☐ ☐ ☐ ☐

2 Identify the pattern in the sentences above and form similar sentences with the words below.

(1) 果汁：____________________

(2) 饭　：____________________

(3) 问题：____________________

Go400 **WANT TO LEARN MORE?**

Check out the Text > Reading section in the Go400 CD.

Text 2

Read the following text carefully.

今天我们全家一起吃中餐(zhōng cān)。我们坐在圆桌旁，爷爷奶奶坐在一起，爸爸妈妈坐在爷爷奶奶两边，我和哥哥坐在妈妈旁边。

我们每个人有一双筷子(kuài zi)、一个汤匙(tāng chí)和一碗(wǎn)饭，桌上有四盘(pán)菜和一碗汤(wǎn tāng)。我们用筷子(kuài zi)，一边吃饭，一边吃菜。爷爷说："吃饭不要快(kuài)*，要一口(kǒu)一口(kǒu)慢慢(màn màn)吃。"

大家吃饱后，我帮妈妈把碗筷(wǎn kuài)*拿到厨房。

*快 quick, fast　*碗筷 (referring to tableware here)

Answer these questions in Chinese.

1 According to the author, what is the seating arrangement at the table? Check the box next to the correct seating plan below.

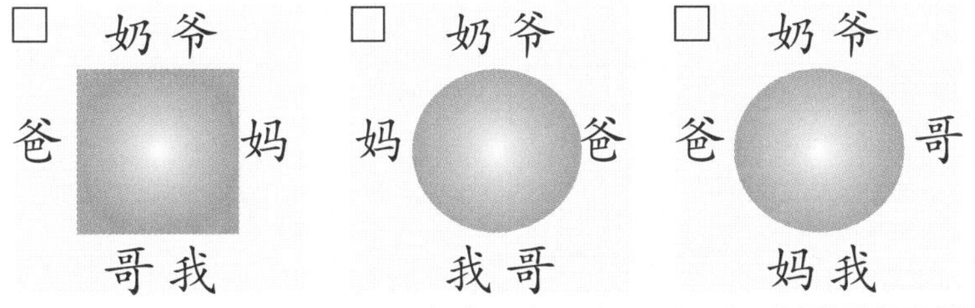

2 What utensils did the author use for his meal?

3 What did the author eat for this meal?

Let's DO IT

1 Use the Internet to find out the proper table setting for a Chinese and Western meal respectively.
2 In small groups, identify the errors in the pictures below and write them down.

A

B

C

What are the errors in each of the pictures?

A ____________________

B ____________________

C ____________________

3 Apart from what you have corrected in these pictures, what other etiquette should we follow when dining in a Chinese or Western setting? Share the information with your class.

LEARNING LOG

I can...	Excellent	Good	Fair	Needs Improvement
1 name the tableware used in Chinese and Western dining such as knife, fork, chopsticks, etc.	☐	☐	☐	☐
2 use "把……" to describe the action imposed on an object and the result of that action on the object.	☐	☐	☐	☐
3 recognize that "好" is used before an adjective to express it to a greater degree.	☐	☐	☐	☐
4 use "碗" and "盘" as measure words, and use appropriate measure words on various items of tableware.	☐	☐	☐	☐
5 write "刀", "叉", "盘", "把", and "慢".	☐	☐	☐	☐

LESSON 8

怎么去？

How Do I Go?

My Goals

1 Be able to state the mode of transportation by which I would like to travel

2 Be able to use "先……再……" to express the sequence of two events

3 Be able to state the exclusive conditions under which a goal may be achieved

4 Be able to recognize that characters which contain "走" are related to movement

5 Become familiar with the names of common modes of transportation

Get Started

qì chē
汽车

chū zū chē　jì chéng chē
出租车/计程车

gōng jiāo chē　gōng chē
公交车/公车

mó tuō chē　jī chē
摩托车/机车
(motorcycle)

dì tiě
地铁

huǒ chē
火车
(train)

fēi jī
飞机

chuán
船
(ship)

gǎn de shàng
赶得上

gǎn bu shàng
赶不上
(unable to make it in time)

Play It

1. Discuss the modes of transportation introduced on this page and the possible verbs that can accompany them, such as "坐", "开", and "买".
2. The participants stand in a row to play the game. The teacher will first state a mode of transportation. The first student in line must answer, "Subject + an accompanying verb + 的", followed by another mode of transportation for the next student to respond in the same format. Note that the subject must change between each turn in the sequence of "你", "我", and "他".
3. During the game, everybody claps to create a tempo and the participants respond to the rhythm.
4. A participant is disqualified if he fails to keep up with the rhythm, uses the incorrect subject or verb, or is not able to respond. The last student remaining in the game wins.

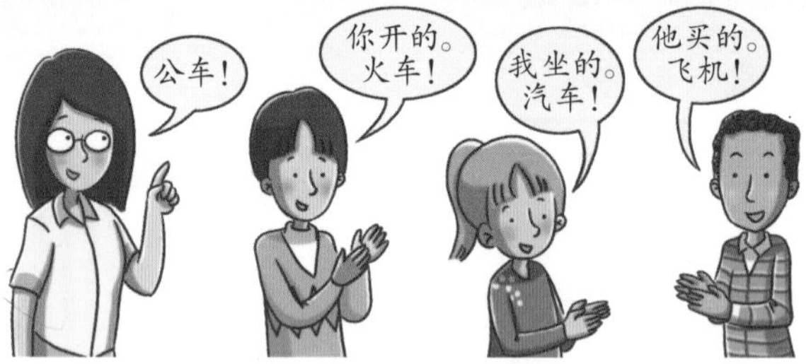

New Words

qì chē 汽车 vehicle	chū zū chē jì chéng chē 出租车/计程车 taxi	gōng jiāo chē gōng chē 公交车/公车 bus	dì tiě 地铁 subway
fēi jī 飞机 airplane	gǎn de shàng 赶得上 make it in time		

Let's CHANT

Go400

dā fēi jī dì tiě
搭飞机，坐地铁，

gōng chē
我坐公车你开车，

jì chéng chē
路上还有计程车，

gǎn gǎn jiāo tōng
赶来赶去交通忙。

TIP "搭" and "坐" are verbs that describe being in or on a vehicle. While they are used interchangeably in most cases, only "坐" can be used to describe a ride on a motorcycle.

Match It

The same type of vehicle may be known by different terms in different areas. In some cases, the term may even be coined from an English word. All of the following words refer to public buses and taxis. Classify them and write their corresponding letters under the correct picture.

☐ ☐

☐ ☐ ☐ ☐

(A) 公车

(B) 出租车

gōng gòng qì chē
(C) 公共汽车

(D) 计程车

(E) 公交车

bā shì
(F) 巴士

New Words

dā
搭 take (a vehicle)

gǎn
赶 rush

jiāo tōng
交通 traffic

Let's Learn GRAMMAR

xiān
先……再……

TIP
The construction "先……再……", which means "first…then…", expresses the sequence of two actions. The first action is placed after "先", while the later action is placed after "再".

xiān
你先走，我再走。

xiān
他先进教室，你再进教室。

xiān
大家要先洗手再吃饭。

xiān
你先写作业再洗澡。

xiān
妈妈今天很忙，早上她先去买菜，再去医院看奶奶。

zhōng guó　xiān　dì tiě　jī chǎng
我明天要去中国(China)旅行，我要先坐地铁去机场，

fēi jī　zhōng guó
再坐飞机去中国。

New Words

xiān
先 first

jī chǎng
机场 airport

cái
才

dì tiě cái kuài
早上车多，上学要坐地铁才快。

chū zū chē cái gǎn de shàng
快八点了，你得坐出租车才赶得上。

cái
用筷子吃饭，要多练习才用得好。

huǒ chē fēi jī cái kuài
你坐火车太慢了，坐飞机才快。

TIP For the examples on the left, "才" indicates that a result can only be achieved under certain conditions.

Phrasal Verb
Verb 来 Verb 去

chē zhàn
小明走来走去，还是不知道车站在哪里。

我看来看去，不知道要选哪一本书。

棒球比赛赢了，大家开心地跳来跳去。

TIP "Verb 来 Verb 去" is a common phrasal verb that expresses the repetition of an action.

New Words

cái
才 then, just

kuài
快 fast

chē zhàn
车站 station

Go400 **WANT TO LEARN MORE?**

Check out the Text > Sentence Pattern section in the Go400 CD.

Let's TALK

Find a partner and practice the following dialogues.

Task 1

A: 我五点要到餐厅，坐公交车(gōng jiāo chē)赶得上(gǎn de shàng)吗？

B: 赶不上(gǎn bu shàng)，你要坐出租车(chū zū chē)才(cái)赶得上(gǎn de shàng)。

A: 从这里到餐厅要多久(duō jiǔ)(how long)？

B: 坐出租车(chū zū chē)要半个小时。

A: 请你帮我叫车(jiào chē)(call for a taxi)好吗？

B: 好的。

Task 2

A: 公交车(gōng jiāo chē)怎么还不来？

B: 你等几路公交车(gōng jiāo chē)？

A: 我等五十二路公交车(gōng jiāo chē)。我等了三十分钟了，等来等去，还是等不到。

B: 我想你得坐出租车(chū zū chē)了。

A: 我只有十块钱，不够坐出租车(chū zū chē)的。

TIP Many public buses are labeled with various numbers to indicate the different routes they take. In Chinese, one might say "O 路公交车" or "O 号公交车", depending on the area he/she is in.

Task 3

A: 请问去图书馆要坐什么车？

dì tiě gōng chē dì tiě

B: 你可以坐地铁，也可以坐公交车。坐地铁比坐

gōng jiāo chē kuài

公交车快。

dì tiě zhàn

A: 我想坐地铁。请问我要坐到哪一站下车？

zhàn

B: 你要坐到公园站下车。下车后再向右转，

走五分钟就到了。

A: 谢谢！

Task 4

A: ______________________________

dì tiě dì tiě zhàn

B: 你可以坐地铁。从地铁站出来，

diàn yǐng yuàn

就可以看见电影院 (movie theater) 了。

A: ______________________________

kuài gǎn de shàng

B: 你要快一点儿，才赶得上。

The following dialogues are adapted from the dialogues in the Text > Dialogue section in your Go400.
Listen to the CD before reading the transcript on this page.

Task 5

A: 你怎么去上学？

dì tiě
B: 我坐地铁去上学。

Task 6

dā fēi jī
A: 你搭几点的飞机？

dā fēi jī jī chǎng
B: 我搭下午三点的飞机，下午一点就得到机场。

Task 7

zhuǎn chē
A: 你去上学要转车吗？

zhuǎn chē dā gōng chē zhuǎn dì tiě
B: 要转车，我先搭二路公车，再转地铁。

Task 8

jiào jì chéng chē
A: 你要叫计程车吗？

gǎn jī chǎng dā fēi jī
B: 是的，我要赶去机场搭飞机，

jiào jì chéng chē
请帮我打电话叫计程车。

New Words

zhuǎn chē
转车 transfer (from a vehicle to another)

Let's Learn CHARACTER

Apart from animals, common modes of transportation include cars on land, boats on water, and planes in the air. The characters "车", "船 (chuán)", and "飞 (fēi)" are closely related to the illustrations of related concepts, as shown below.

→ 车

"车" looks like a cart used for carrying heavy goods.

→ 舟 (zhōu)

The left component of "船 (chuán)" is "舟 (zhōu)", which means "small boat".

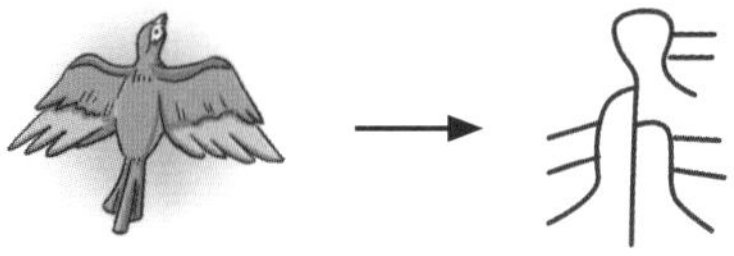

→ 飞 (fēi)

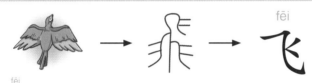

"飞 (fēi)" looks like a bird soaring in the sky with its wings spread out.

Besides "车", "船 (chuán)", and "飞 (fēi)", characters containing "走" are also commonly related to movement.

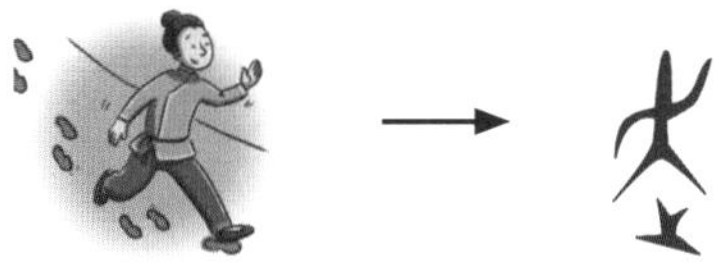

→ 走

"走" is derived historically from the illustration of a figure jogging while swinging his arms by his sides. The lower component of the character resembles a foot.

Practice It

Do you know any words that contain the component "走"? Write them down.

走		

Let's READ

Text 1

Read the following text carefully.

公车(gōng chē)上，什么人都有：男的，女的，老的，小的，高的，矮的，胖的，瘦的。

有的人站*(zhàn)着，有的人坐着；有的人睡觉，有的人看书，有的人听歌*(tīng gē)，有的人吃东西，有的人看外面，有的人打电话，有的人和旁边的人说话*(shuō huà)；有的人大声*(dà shēng)说，有的人轻声*(qīng shēng)笑。

每一站**(zhàn)，有不同的人下车，每一站(zhàn)，有不同的人上车；每个人，从不同的地方*(dì fang)来，每个人，到不同的地方(dì fang)去。

*站 stand　*听歌 listen to songs　*说话 speak　*大声 loudly　*轻声 softly　** 站 stop; station　*地方 place

Answer these questions in Chinese.

1 Which of the following sentences do not accurately reflect the content of the passage?

□ 公车上大家都做一样的事。
□ 大家都在同一个车站上车。
□ 每一站都有人上车、下车。

2 According to the passage, what do the people do while traveling on the public bus?

Go400

WANT TO LEARN MORE?

Check out the Text > Reading section in the Go400 CD.

Text 2

Read the following text carefully.

上个星期天是爷爷七十岁生日，爸爸送了两张机(jī)票(piào)*给爷爷，请爷爷带奶奶去香港(xiāng gǎng)*玩。

爷爷说：“这是最好的生日礼物，到香港(xiāng gǎng)可以去看朋友，可以去买东西，还可以去吃美食(měi shí)*。”

爷爷还说，那天爸爸要上班，我们要上学，所以不用送他们去机场(jī chǎng)。他和奶奶先(xiān)坐公交车(gōng jiāo chē)再转(zhuǎn)地铁(dì tiě)，只要四十分钟就可以到机场(jī chǎng)了。

可是爸爸不放心(fàng xīn)*，还是开车送爷爷奶奶去机场(jī chǎng)了。

*机票 air ticket　*香港 Hong Kong
*美食 delicacy　*放心 be at ease

Answer these questions in Chinese.

1 What does the author's grandfather wish to do in Hong Kong?

2 In the passage, the author mentions many ways to get to the airport. What are they?

3 Which of the following phrases is the most suitable title for this passage?

☐ 自己去机场　☐ 爷爷的生日礼物　☐ 快乐的旅行

Let's DO IT

1 Plan a vacation and prepare your itinerary on presentation slides. Present your itinerary to your class. Your presentation should also include the following topics:

❶ 你要去哪里旅行？
❷ 你什么时候要去旅行？
❸ 你要和谁一起去？
❹ 那里天气怎么样？
❺ 你怎么去那里？
❻ 旅行的时候，你想做什么？

2 During your classmates' presentations, listen and record the mode of transportation that two of your classmates will be taking to their destinations.

Name	Vacation Plans
1	
2	

LEARNING LOG

I can...

	Excellent	Good	Fair	Needs Improvement
1 name common modes of transportation.	☐	☐	☐	☐
2 describe how to get to my destination by various modes of transportation.	☐	☐	☐	☐
3 use "先……再……" to express the sequence of two actions.	☐	☐	☐	☐
4 use "才" to state that a result can only be achieved under certain conditions.	☐	☐	☐	☐
5 write "飞", "机", "先", "才", and "赶".	☐	☐	☐	☐

LESSON 9

我们的大地
The Earth

My Goals

1 Be able to describe if our environment is clean as well as ways to preserve our environment
2 Be familiar with the use of ordinal numbers
3 Be able to use "只有……，才……" to indicate that a result can only be achieved under the stated conditions
4 Be able to differentiate between different word classes
5 Become familiar with words associated with the environment

Get Started

shān
山
(mountain)

hǎi yáng
海洋
(ocean)

cǎo yuán
草原
(grassland)

shā mò
沙漠
(desert)

chéng shì
城市
(city)

gān jìng
干净

ān jìng
安静

shū fu
舒服

zāng
脏

chǎo
吵

难过

Play It

1 Create vocabulary cards using the adjectives introduced on this page. Stick them face down on the board.
2 Divide the class into two teams.
3 Representatives from each team take turns to locate opposite words by flipping two cards over at once. If the words are indeed opposites, the student must read the words aloud before he/she is awarded a point and is allowed to continue by flipping two more cards. The team with the most points wins. Vocabulary cards that were used in previous lessons may be included in the game for increased difficulty.

New Words

gān jìng
干净 clean

zāng
脏 dirty

ān jìng
安静 quiet

chǎo
吵 noisy

shū fu
舒服 comfortable

Let's CHANT

Go 400

dà dì
大地是你我的家，

也是动物们的家，

ān quán gān jìng zāng luàn
安全干净不脏乱，

大家健康又快乐。

Learn and Share

The Earth is home to both humans and animals. However, there are many species of animals which are on the brink of extinction today. These animals, such as China's Giant Panda, need our protection.

The Giant Pandas, with their specialized diet of mainly bamboo shoots, have a low reproduction rate and do not defend themselves well against predators. Much of their habitat has also been wiped out by man's urbanization efforts. As a result, there are few Giant Pandas left in the wild, and they have become China's top protected species.

On the Internet, research on other endangered animals in the world today. What can we do to protect them from extinction?

New Words

dà dì
大地 the Earth

ān quán
安全 safe

zāng luàn
脏乱 dirty and disorderly

Let's Learn GRAMMAR

dì
第 + Numeral + (Measure Word)

> **TIP** "第 + numeral" indicates an ordinal number. It is often used with a measure word.

guò mǎ lù　　　zhù yì　　　ān quán dì
过马路(cross the road)要注意车子，安全第一。

dì
这是我第一次自己坐飞机，很紧张。

dì
我有一个堂哥，我是爷爷奶奶的第二个孙子。

dì　míng
这次比赛我们得了第一名，大家开心得又叫又跳。

Verb + 着

dà dì
书上写着：大地是你我的家。

票上写着：电影晚上七点开始。

我房间的门开着，你可以自己进去。

> **TIP** In Level Go300, we learned that "verb + 着" indicates that an action is on-going, or that two actions are happening simultaneously. On this page, however, "verb + 着" indicates a state of affairs, which remains unchanged at the point of utterance.

New Words

dì
第 (used before numerals to form ordinal numbers)

zhù yì
注意 (pay) attention

dì　míng
第……名 the rank in a competition

只有	多练习，	才	容易学会。

luàn diū　　gān jìng
只有大家不乱丢东西，地上才会干净。

gān jìng
只有大家一起把房间清理干净，

shū fu
我们才能住得舒服。

TIP The sentence structure "只有……，才……" differs slightly from "只要……，就……". "只有……，才……" indicates that a particular condition, and no other, must be met before the desired result can be achieved.

"只要……，就……" indicates that the desired result can be achieved as long as certain conditions are met. Other conditions may be included as well. This sentence structure shows that the speaker does not find this task very difficult.

只要	多练习，	就	容易学会。

luàn diū　　gān jìng
只要大家不乱丢东西，地上就会干净。

gān jìng　　shū fu
只要把房间清理干净，我们就能住得舒服。

yì si
只要你用心想，就能知道这句话的意思。

New Words

luàn diū
乱丢 to litter about

yì si
意思 meaning

Go400 WANT TO LEARN MORE?

Check out the Text > Sentence Pattern section in the Go400 CD.

Let's TALK

Find a partner and practice the following dialogues.

Task 1

A: 妈，我回来了。我的衣服脏(zāng)了。

B: 衣服脏(zāng)了没关系，洗衣机(xǐ yī jī)(washing machine)可以洗得很干净(gān jìng)。你先去洗手，再来吃东西。

A: 我的手不脏(zāng)，可以不洗吗？

B: 吃东西前要先洗洗手，健康第(dì)一。

Task 2

A: 哥哥常常生病，这个星期他又生病了。

B: 我早上看到他出去了，他怎么不在家里休息？

A: 他不舒服(shū fu)，可是还得去上班。

B: 他要多运动，才不会生病。

Task 3

A：这是我第(dì)一次参加这个活动，我要做什么？

B：我们只要把草地上的垃圾(lā jī)(litter)清理干净(gān jìng)，就可以了。

A：清理完，我们就有干净(gān jìng)的草地了。

B：只有大家不乱丢(luàn diū)东西，我们才能有干净(gān jìng)的大(dà)地(dì)。地上不脏乱(zāng luàn)，你我都开心。

Task 4

A：这是我第(dì)一次开车。

B：请你注意(zhù yì)安全(ān quán)，开车要小心。

A：我会的。我不开快车，安全(ān quán)最重要。

B：没错，安全第(ān quán dì)一。

The following dialogues can be found in the Text > Dialogue section in your Go400. Listen to the CD before reading the transcript on this page.

Task 5

A: 我的车停在这里安全（ān quán）吗？

B: 没问题。

Task 6

A: 那家餐厅干净（gān jìng）吗？

B: 还不错，我常常去那家餐厅吃饭。

Task 7

A: 你在做什么？

B: 我在清理地上的脏（zāng）东西。

New Words

乱（luàn） disorderly

Task 8

A: 你明天会去城（chéng）里参加活动吗？

B: 我不去，城（chéng）里人多车也多，太脏（zāng）太乱（luàn）又太吵（chǎo）。

Let's Learn PHRASE

Understanding the word class of Chinese words is important because the word class determines the usage of a word, as well as its placement in a sentence. Can you differentiate the following words by their word class? Classify them into the boxes below.

A 吃

B 慢

C 床

D 中餐

E gān jìng 干净

F 筷子

G shū fu 舒服

H 睡觉

Noun	Verb	Adjective

Want More Practice?

Identify new vocabulary in your Go400 book. In your class, take turns to classify them into the various word classes.

Practice It

The following is a sentence expansion exercise. Model after the example on the right. Pay attention to the placement of the words in different word classes.

中餐

____

____

____

____

EXAMPLE

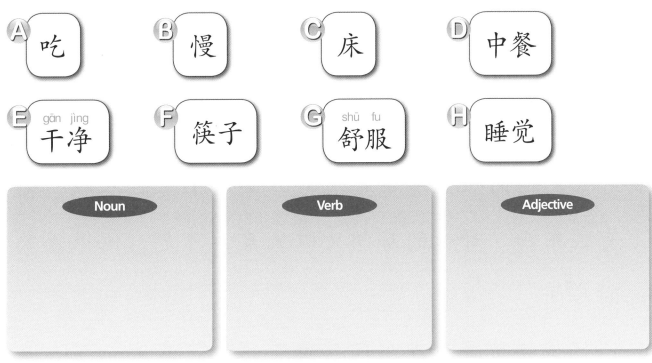

睡觉
在床上 睡觉
在干净的床上 睡觉
在干净的床上舒服地睡觉
我在干净的床上舒服地睡觉。

Let's READ

Text 1

Read the following text carefully.

哥哥不爱干净(gān jìng)，他很少清理房间。

他的门关(guān)*着，门上写着：我自己的小天地，请不要进来！他的床上有书也有笔，桌子上有脏(zāng)衣服，地上有脏(zāng)东西。哥哥的房间又脏(zāng)又乱(luàn)，可是，他很喜欢他的房间。

妈妈要哥哥清理房间，哥哥说："我太忙了，我没有时间清理。"姐姐要帮哥哥清理房间，哥哥说："不要！不要！我的房间很乱(luàn)，可是很舒服(shū fu)。你一清理，我就找不到我的东西了。"

*关 close

Answer these questions in Chinese.

1 Does Older Brother welcome everyone to his room? Why? No, he doesn't like cleaning

2 Does Older Brother want someone else to clean his room for him? Why? Yes

3 The author has an Older Sister who is neat and tidy. Model after the first and second paragraphs to introduce her older sister's room. Read the passage in the CD to find out the differences between the passage and your writing.

Text 2

Read the following text carefully.

上个星期天我们全家(quán jiā)*一起去公园玩。那一天是晴天，不冷也不热。公园里的花都开得很美丽，树也长得又高又大。

在公园里，我们看到小鸟在天上(tiān shàng)*飞，小朋友在树下玩，大人在附近跑步，还有一个老人(lǎo rén)*坐在椅子上看书，两只小猫在椅子下睡觉。

公园很干净(gān jìng)，没有小狗的大小便，也没有垃圾(lā jī)*。我可以在草地上跳舞，也可以对着小花唱歌。看着干净(gān jìng)的大地(dà dì)真舒服(shū fu)！我爱这个公园，我会常常来玩。

*全家 whole family　*天上 in the sky　*老人 the elderly　*垃圾 litter

Answer these questions in Chinese.

1 What did the author see at the park? Where exactly did he see them?
2 Does the author like the park? How do you know?
3 Do you go to the park? How is the park you frequent like? What do you do at the park?

Go400

WANT TO LEARN MORE?

Check out the Text > Reading section in the Go400 CD.

Let's DO IT

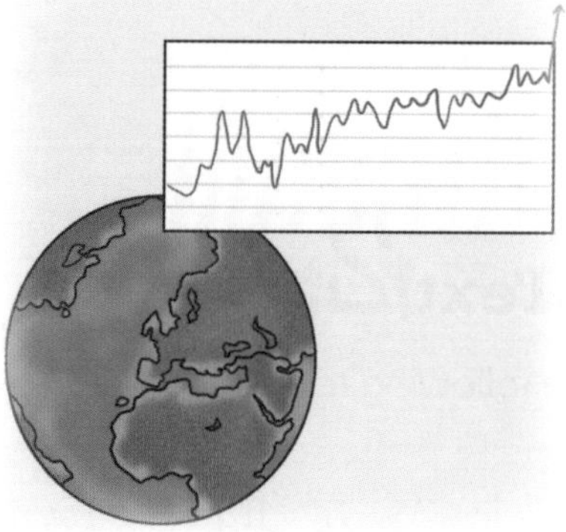

1 Is our Earth in peril? Gather data from the news or the Internet to show the problems that the planet Earth is facing.

2 What can we do to save the Earth? Think of four ways to save the Earth, and present them to the class in presentation slides.

1

2

3

4

LEARNING LOG

I can...	Excellent	Good	Fair	Needs Improvement
1 describe the environment using words such as "脏乱" and "干净".	☐	☐	☐	☐
2 describe ways to keep the environment clean.	☐	☐	☐	☐
3 recognize that "第 + numeral" indicates an ordinal number.	☐	☐	☐	☐
4 use the sentence structures "只有……，才……" and "只要……，就……" appropriately.	☐	☐	☐	☐
5 differentiate Chinese words by their word classes.	☐	☐	☐	☐
6 write "注", "意", "思", "舒", and "全".	☐	☐	☐	☐

LESSON

10 工作天地

Work and Occupations

My Goals

1 Be able to talk about my ambitions, and display a good work attitude
2 Be able to express the possibility of two situations
3 Be able to rewrite sentences without changing the syntactic word order
4 Be able to use the pause mark " 、" appropriately
5 Become familiar with the names of common occupations

Get Started

yǎn yuán
演员

jǐng yuán
警员

yùn dòng yuán
运动员

diàn yuán
店员

yī shī
医师 / 医生

lǜ shī
律师

gōng chéng shī
工程师

chú shī
厨师
(chef)

jūn rén
军人
(soldier)

nóng mín
农民
(farmer)

gōng rén
工人
(worker)

Survey and Discuss

1 Interview your family and friends. Find out what the most popular occupation is among them.

2 What do you think the most popular occupation will be 15 years from now? Give reasons for your view.

New Words

gōng zuò 工作 work	tiān dì 天地 world	yǎn yuán 演员 actor	jǐng yuán 警员 police officer	yùn dòng yuán 运动员 (professional) athlete
diàn yuán 店员 sales clerk	yī shī 医师 doctor	lǜ shī 律师 lawyer	gōng chéng shī 工程师 engineer	

Let's CHANT

Go 400

lǜ shī gōng chéng shī
医生律师工程师，

yǎn yuán jǐng yuán yùn dòng yuán
演员警员运动员，

zhí yè
职业没有好和坏，

xìng qù
自己兴趣最重要。

TIP

Historically in China, teachers were highly regarded because they held a paramount role in transmitting knowledge through the generations. To the Chinese who revered nature and valued ethics and principles, teachers were highly honored, as were the skies (天), the earth (地), the emperor (君 jūn), and one's ancestors (亲 qīn). Sacrifices were even made to teachers just like how sacrifices were offered to Gods and ancestors. The distinction given to teachers is still evident today where the names of many respectable occupations such as lawyer (律师) and engineer (工程师) contain the character "师", from the word "teacher" (老师).

New Words

zhí yè
职业 occupation

xìng qù
兴趣 interest

Let's Learn GRAMMAR

yì zhí
一直

yì zhí gōng zuò
舅舅一直找不到工作。

yùn dòng yuán
堂哥是运动员，他每天从早上

yì zhí
七点一直练习到下午四点。

yì zhí
你从这里一直向前走，就可以

到图书馆了。

TIP "一直" is an adverbial. "一直 + verb/adj." shows that an action or situation goes on and on.
"一直+ verb + 到" is typically followed by a phrase indicating the extent of the action, or the location or time at which the action ends.
"一直" also means to keep going in a direction, which is usually stated after the verb or the phrase "一直".

New Words

yì zhí 一直 continuously	huò 或 or

huò
或

huò
星期五或星期六我都可以去看电影。

huò
去图书馆很方便，你要坐公交车或坐地铁都可以。

huò
我要吃面，请给我一双筷子或一个叉子。

gōng zuò shàng wǎng huò
你想找工作，可以上网 (surf the Internet)或

请朋友帮忙。

TIP "或" is a conjunction which means "or". It indicates that one has to make a choice between two or more options. It is different from "和", which is a conjunction that means "and".

Sentence Transformation: Placing the Subject at the Beginning of the Sentence

gōng zuò
太累的工作，他不想做。

gōng zuò
→ 他不想做太累的工作。

jǐng yuán zhí yè
警员是弟弟最喜欢的职业。

zhí yè jǐng yuán
→ 弟弟最喜欢的职业是警员。

xìng qù
音乐是我最有兴趣的学科。

xìng qù
→ 我最有兴趣的学科是音乐。

xū yào 需要

xū yào
我需要电脑才能做今天的功课。

xū yào
奶奶生病了，需要我们去照顾她。

yǎn yuán xū yào xìng qù
做演员很辛苦，需要有兴趣才行。

xū yào
你需要谁帮忙？

TIP "需要" may be used as a verb or a noun. As a noun, "需要" means "one's needs" as in "每个人的需要都不一样，你要先问，再去做。". In this lesson, we focus more on "需要" as a verb, where it means "require" or "need".

New Words

xū yào
需要 need, require

Go400 WANT TO LEARN MORE?

Check out the Text > Sentence Pattern section in the Go400 CD.

Let's TALK

Find a partner and practice the following dialogues.

Task 1

A: 放暑假了，我想去打工。

B: 你想去哪里打工？

A: 我对学校的工作(gōng zuò)有兴趣(xìng qù)。

B: 你可以请老师帮忙问问看，或(huò)请在学校打工的同学帮忙找找看。

A: 大关的哥哥就在学校图书馆工作(gōng zuò)，他说明天要带我去那里看一看。

Task 2

A: 你妈妈的职业(zhí yè)是什么？

B: 我妈妈是律师(lǜ shī)。

A: 你爸爸也是律师(lǜ shī)吗？

B: 不是，他是厨师(chú shī)。下个星期我们要去他的餐厅吃饭，你要不要一起去？

Task 3

gōng zuò
A: 你爸爸在医院工作累不累？

gōng zuò　gōng zuò
B: 爸爸的工作很辛苦，有时晚上也得工作。

bái tiān　gōng zuò
A: 你爸爸不能白天 (in the day) 工作，晚上休息吗？

xū yào　yī shī
B: 不能，因为只要医院需要帮忙，医师就得去。

yǎn yuán　bái tiān　gōng zuò
A: 我姐姐是演员，她白天晚上也都要工作。

zhí yè　gōng zuò
B: 每一种职业都很辛苦，每一种工作都不容易。

Task 4

xìng qù
A: 你的兴趣是什么？

B: ______________________________

yǐ hòu　gōng zuò
A: 你以后 (later on) 想做什么工作？

B: ______________________________

A: 为什么？

B: ______________________________

Task 5

Rearrange the following sentences to form a coherent dialogue. In the right order, write down the corresponding letters in the boxes below. When this is done, you may listen to the Text > Dialogue Section in your Go 400 for the correct answer.

❶ 从星期一到星期五，我每天工作(gōng zuò)八个小时。

❷ 我在医院工作(gōng zuò)。

❸ 你在哪里工作(gōng zuò)？

❹ 你暑假要去哪里玩？

❺ 你在医院做什么工作(gōng zuò)？

❻ 我暑假要工作(gōng zuò)，没有时间(shí jiān)(time)去玩。

❼ 你每天都要上班吗？

❽ 医院有__________，我会说中文，我可以帮他们的忙。

→

Let's Learn PUNCTUATION

、

dùn hào
顿号 (pause mark)

In Chinese, the pause mark "、", also known as an enumeration comma, is used to indicate slight pauses within a sentence or between words in a series of words. When a phrase is composed of two or more parts, the first parts are typically separated by pause marks while the final two parts are joined by a conjunction such as "和". The pause mark in Chinese is written the same way as one of the strokes in Chinese characters —— the dot (点 diǎn, "丶").

书房是哥哥的天地(tiān dì)，除了爸妈、姐姐和我，谁都不能进去。

工程师(gōng chéng shī)、演员(yǎn yuán)和工人(gōng rén)，每一种职业(zhí yè)都很重要。

中文、数学、史地、音乐和体育，每一科都要认真地学。

Practice It

Since Level Go200, we have learned a number of punctuation marks. Can you recall what these punctuation marks are and their uses? Fill in the blanks below with the appropriate punctuation marks.

1. 书上写着☐大地(dà dì)是你我的家☐
2. 这个问题我不会☐这个句子是什么意思☐
3. 晴天☐我们在运动场跑步☐雨天☐我们在体育馆打球☐
4. 公交车☐地铁和出租车都可以到学校☐你要坐哪一个☐

Let's READ

Text 1

Read the following text carefully.

暑假到了，哥哥和姐姐开始找工作(gōng zuò)。

哥哥去很多地方(dì fang)*找工作(gōng zuò)，医院、图书馆、市场，还有商店(shāng diàn)*，他都去过。辛苦的工作(gōng zuò)，他不要；钱少的工作(gōng zuò)，他不要；周末的工作(gōng zuò)，他也不要；找了很久，他一直(yì zhí)找不到工作(gōng zuò)。

姐姐也去很多地方(dì fang)找工作(gōng zuò)，除了自己找工作(gōng zuò)，她还请朋友帮她找。

姐姐说："赚钱多或(huò)赚钱少，没关系，工作时间(gōng zuò shí jiān)*长或工作时间(huò gōng zuò shí jiān)短也没关系，我想做做看。"

很快地，姐姐就找到了工作(gōng zuò)。

*地方 place　*商店 store　*时间 time

Answer these questions in Chinese.

1 What kind of job is Older Brother looking for?

2 How did Older Sister manage to find a job so easily?

3 Which of the following sentences does not accurately reflect the content of the passage?

□ 姐姐想找工作时间长的工作。

□ 姐姐比哥哥早找到工作。

□ 哥哥不想在周末工作。

> **TIP** The same occupation may be known by different terms in different areas. For example, a doctor may be known as "医生" or "医师". A teacher may be known as "老师" or "教师". A police officer may be known as "警员" or "警察".

Text 2

Read the following text carefully.

每个人都需要(xū yào)别人帮忙，每个人也都可以帮忙别人。

律师(lǜ shī)、老师、店员(diàn yuán)、警员(jǐng yuán)生病了，都需要(xū yào)医生帮忙看病。医生自己生病了，也要找别的医生看病。

每个人都很重要。我们想看一场好电影，就要有好的演员(yǎn yuán)；我们想看一场好球赛，就要有好的球员(qiú yuán)*。

每个人都很重要，每个人都需要(xū yào)别人帮忙，每个人也可以帮别人的忙。

*球员 player

Answer these questions in Chinese.

1 How many occupations are mentioned in the passage? What are they?
2 Who does the doctor go to when he falls sick?
3 Why do we need good actors and good players?
4 Listen to this passage on the CD. Which sentences are different? Do the passages mean the same?

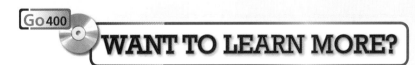

Go400 **WANT TO LEARN MORE?**

Check out the Text > Reading section in the Go400 CD.

Let's DO IT

Imagine the person you will be in 15 years. Write a letter to that person, telling her what you wish would be different in 15 years. Incorporate the topics below in your letter by making brief notes in the mind map. Elaborate on the points in your letter and type it out.

十五年后是__________年，那个时候的我……

每天最重要的事是什么？

放假时做什么？

zhí yè
职业是什么？

有哪些家人？

LEARNING LOG

I can...	Excellent	Good	Fair	Needs Improvement
1 name common occupations such as lawyer, engineer, doctor, etc.	☐	☐	☐	☐
2 talk about my ambitions and give reasons for my ambitions.	☐	☐	☐	☐
3 use "或", "一直", and "需要" appropriately in sentences.	☐	☐	☐	☐
4 rearrange transposed sentences such that the subject appears in the beginning of the sentence, without altering the meaning of the original sentence.	☐	☐	☐	☐
5 use the pause mark "、" appropriately in sentences to indicate halting pauses.	☐	☐	☐	☐
6. write "店", "或", "兴", "趣", and "直".	☐	☐	☐	☐

Vocabulary Index

Words indicated with an asterisk (*) are supplementary vocabulary from each lesson. They are included to supplement students' vocabulary and enhance their oral proficiency.

Pinyin	Simplified Character	English	Traditional Character	Lesson
A				
ān jìng	安静	quiet	安靜	L9
ān quán	安全	safe	安全	L9
B				
bǎ	把	(used before an object and followed by a verb)		L7
bǎ	把	(a measure word for knife, etc.)		L7
bàn gōng shì	办公室	office	辦公室	L1
bāng	帮	help	幫	L3
bāng máng	帮忙	help	幫忙	L3
bié	别	don't	別	L5
bié de	别的	other	別的	L5
bié rén	别人	other people	別人	L5
bú cuò	不错	not bad; good	不錯	L2
C				
cái	才	then, just		L8
cān tīng	餐厅	dining hall, cafeteria	餐廳	L1
cǎo yuán	草原*	grassland	草原	L9
cè suǒ	厕所	restroom	廁所	L1
chā zi	叉子	fork		L7
chǎo	吵	noisy		L9
chē zhàn	车站	station	車站	L8
chéng shì	城市*	city		L9
chū zū chē	出租车	taxi	出租車	L8
chú fáng	厨房	come out	廚房	L6
chú shī	厨师 *	chef	廚師	L10
chuán	船	ship		L8
chūn jià	春假	spring break		L5
cuò	错	wrong	錯	L2

D				
dā	搭	take (a vehicle)	搭	L8
dǎ gōng	打工	have a part-time job		L5
dà dì	大地	the Earth		L9
dà lóu	大楼	building	大樓	L1
dà xiǎo biàn	大小便	feces and urine		L4
dāo zi	刀子	knife		L7
de	地	(a particle used after an adverbial)		L2
dì	第	(used before numerals to form ordinal numbers)		L9
dì...míng	第……名	the rank in a competition		L9
dì lǐ	地理	Geography		L2
dì tiě	地铁	subway	地鐵	L8
diàn yuán	店员	sales clerk	店員	L10
dōng biān	东边	east	東邊	L6
dōng xi	东西	thing	東西	L6
dòng wù	动物	animal	動物	L4
dòng wù yuán	动物园	zoo	動物園	L4
F				
fàn tīng	饭厅	dining room	飯廳	L6
fáng jiān	房间	room	房間	L6
fàng	放	put		L7
fàng (jià)	放(假)	take day(s) off		L5
fēi jī	飞机	airplane	飛機	L8
G				
gān jìng	干净	clean	乾淨	L9
gǎn	赶	rush	趕	L8
gǎn bu shàng	赶不上*	unable to make it in time	趕不上	L8
gǎn de shàng	赶得上	make it in time	趕得上	L8
gèng	更	more (+ adj.)		L3
gōng chē	公车	bus	公車	L8
gōng chéng shī	工程师	engineer	工程師	L10
gōng rén	工人*	worker		L10
gōng jiāo chē	公交车	bus	公交車	L8
gōng yuán	公园	park	公園	L4

gōng zuò	工作	work		L10
gǒu	狗	dog		L4
guō	锅*	pot	鍋	L7
guò shēng rì	过生日	celebrate one's birthday	過生日	L3
H				
hǎi yáng	海洋*	ocean		L9
hán jià	寒假	winter vacation		L5
huā yuán	花园*	garden	花園	L4
huǒ chē	火车*	train	火車	L8
huò	或	or		L10
J				
jī chǎng	机场	airport	機場	L8
jī chē	机车*	motorcycle	機車	L8
jì chéng chē	计程车	taxi	計程車	L8
jià	假	vacation; break; leave		L5
jià qī	假期	vacation		L5
jiān	间	(a measure word for room, house, etc.)	間	L6
jiàn kāng	健康	healthy		L3
jiāo tōng	交通	traffic		L8
jiào shì	教室	classroom		L1
jīng guò	经过	pass by	經過	L6
jǐng yuán	警员	police officer	警員	L10
jūn rén	军人	soldier	軍人	L10
K				
kāi shǐ	开始	start, begin	開始	L2
kē	科	subject		L2
kě ài	可爱	adorable, cute	可愛	L4
kè fáng	客房	guest room	客房	L6
kè rén	客人	guest		L6
kè tīng	客厅	living room	客廳	L6
kē xué	科学	Science	科學	L2
kǒu	口	mouthful		L7
kuài	快	fast		L8
kuài lè	快乐	happy	快樂	L3
kuài zi	筷子	chopsticks		L7

L				
lèi	累	tired		L5
lǐ wù	礼物	gift	禮物	L3
lì shǐ	历史	History	歷史	L2
liàn xí	练习	practice	練習	L2
lóu	楼	story, floor	樓	L1
lóu shàng	楼上	upstairs	樓上	L1
lóu xià	楼下	downstairs	樓下	L1
lǚ xíng	旅行	travel		L5
lǜ shī	律师	lawyer	律師	L10
lù yíng	露营*	camp	露營	L5
luàn	乱	disorderly	亂	L9
luàn diū	乱丢	to litter about	亂丢	L9
M				
màn	慢	slow		L7
māo	猫	cat	貓	L4
měi láo	美劳	Art	美勞	L2
měi shù	美术	Art	美術	L2
mó tuō chē	摩托车*	motorcycle	摩托車	L8
N				
nán	难	difficult	難	L2
niǎo	鸟	bird	鳥	L4
niǎo yuán	鸟园*	bird park; aviary	鳥園	L4
nóng míng	农民*	farmer	農民	L10
P				
pán zi	盘子	plate	盤子	L7
páng biān	旁边	beside, next to	旁邊	L1
Q				
qì chē	汽车	vehicle	汽車	L8
qīn yǒu	亲友	friends and relatives	親友	L5
qīng lǐ	清理	clean		L4
qǐng jìn	请进	please come in	請進	L6
qìng zhù	庆祝	celebrate	庆祝	L3

R				
rèn shi	认识	know	認識	L2
rèn zhēn	认真	take seriously	認真	L2
róng yì	容易	easy		L2
S				
shā mò	沙漠*	desert	沙漠	L9
shān	山*	mountain		L9
shàng chuáng	上床	go to bed		L6
shàng lóu	上楼	(go) up the stairs	上樓	L1
shēn tǐ	身体	body	身體	L3
shēng rì	生日	birthday		L3
shēng dàn jià qī	圣诞假期*	Christmas holidays	聖誕假期	L5
shǐ dì	史地	History and Geography		L2
shū fáng	书房	study	書房	L6
shū fu	舒服	comfortable		L9
shǔ jià	暑假	summer vacation		L5
shù xué	数学	Mathematics	數學	L2
shuì fáng	睡房	bedroom	睡房	L6
shuì jiào	睡觉	sleep	睡覺	L6
T				
tā men	它们	they (referring to animals and objects)	牠們	L4
tāng	汤	soup	湯	L7
tāng chí	汤匙	spoon	湯匙	L7
tāng sháo	汤勺	spoon	湯杓	L7
tǐ yù	体育	Physical Education	體育	L2
tǐ yù guǎn	体育馆	gym	體育館	L1
tiān dì	天地	world		L10
tiáo	条	(a measure word for fish)	條	L4
W				
wǎn	碗	bowl		L7
wèi	喂	feed	餵	L4
X				
xī biān	西边	west	西邊	L6
xī cān	西餐	Western food		L7

xī wàng	希望	hope		L3
xǐ zǎo	洗澡	take a bath		L6
xià lóu	下楼	(go) down the stairs	下樓	L1
xiān	先	first		L8
xiào zhǎng	校长	principal	校長	L1
xiào zhǎng shì	校长室	principal's office	校長室	L1
xīn	新	new		L2
xīn nián jià qī	新年假期*	New Year holidays		L5
xíng	行	can		L5
xìng qù	兴趣	interest	興趣	L10
xū yào	需要	need, require		L10
xué kē	学科	subject	學科	L2
Y				
yǎn yuán	演员	actor	演員	L10
yǎng	养	raise	養	L4
yī shī	医师	doctor	醫師	L10
yì si	意思	meaning		L9
yì zhí	一直	continuously		L10
yīn yuè	音乐	Music	音樂	L2
yú	鱼	fish	魚	L4
yù shì	浴室	bathroom		L6
yùn dòng chǎng	运动场	stadium	運動場	L1
yùn dòng yuán	运动员	(professional) athlete	運動員	L10
Z				
zāng	脏	dirty	髒	L9
zāng luàn	脏乱	dirty and disorderly	髒亂	L9
zhǎng	长	grow	長	L3
zhī	只	(a measure word for animals or birds)	隻	L4
zhī dào	知道	know		L1
zhí yè	职业	occupation	職業	L10
zhǐ yǒu	只有	only		L5
zhōng cān	中餐	Chinese food		L7

zhōu mò	周末	weekend	週末	L5
zhù	祝	wish		L3
zhù fú	祝福	wishes		L3
zhù yì	注意	(pay) attention		L9
zhuǎn chē	转车	transfer (from a vehicle to another)	轉車	L8
zuò	坐	sit		L6